Company's Coming

All-Occasion
Gifts
From Your Kitchen

JEAN PARÉ

SPECIAL OCCASION SERIES

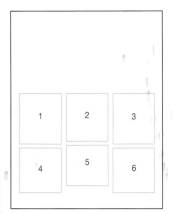

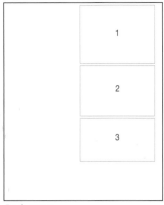

Front cover:

1. Top: Pumpkin Pecan Loaf, page 54
   Bottom: Sesame Snap Cookie Mix, page 54

2. Top: Turkey Chili, page 126
   Bottom: Rustic Apple and Apricot Tart, page 126

3. Sweet Chili Sauce, page 29

4. Cinnamon Spice Popcorn Mix, page 76

5. Raspberry Truffles, page 116

6. Fortune Cookie Favours, page 106

Back cover:

1. Coconut Cashew Candied Popcorn, page 112

2. Clockwise from Left:
   File Folder Card, page 163
   Bouquet Of Cookie Flowers, page 18,
   with Picket Fence Box, page 19,
   Trail Mix Royale, page 18

3. Easter Chick Box, page 17

Second Printing September 2009

Library and Archives Canada Cataloguing in Publication
Paré, Jean, date-
     All-occasion gifts from the kitchen / Jean Paré.
(Special occasion series)
Includes indexes
At head of title: Company's Coming.
ISBN 978-1-897477-04-5
     1. Cookery. 2. Gifts. I. Title. II. Series.
TX652.P352 2009   641.5   C2008-908110-2

Published by
Company's Coming Publishing Limited
2311 – 96 Street
Edmonton, Alberta, Canada T6N 1G3
Tel: 780-450-6223   Fax: 780-450-1857
www.companyscoming.com

Printed in Malaysia

White Wedding Cupcakes, page 108

All-Occasion Gifts From Your Kitchen was created thanks to the dedicated efforts of the people and organizations listed below.

COMPANY'S COMING PUBLISHING LIMITED

Author	Jean Paré
President	Grant Lovig
Vice President, Production & Creative	Alanna Wilson
Research & Development Manager	Jill Corbett
Editorial Director	Tabea Berg
Creative Director	Heather Markham
Editors	Sandra Bit
	Janet Fowler
Senior Food Editor	Lynda Elsenheimer
Food Editors	Mary Anne Korn
	Eleana Yun
Recipe Development Assistant	Stephanie Moore
Researcher	Frieda Lovig
Recipe Editors	Andrea Donini
	Michael Macklon
Contributors	Jennifer Sayers-Bajger
	Patricia Bullock
	Miriam Boody
	Allison Dosman
	Mary Anne Korn
	Eleana Yun
Craft Content Specialist	Paula Bertamini
Copy Editor/Proofreader	Laurie Penner
Editorial Assitant	Brett Bailey
Senior Tester	James Bullock
Testers	Allison Dosman
	Audrey Smetaniuk
Photographer	Stephe Tate Photo
Photography Coordinator/Image Editor	Heather Latimer
Food Stylist	Ashley Billey
Prop Stylist	Snez Ferenac
Prep Assistant	Linda Dobos
Designer	Greg Brown
Nutritionist	Vera Mazurak, Ph.D.

We gratefully acknowledge the following suppliers for their generous support of our Test and Photography Kitchens:

Broil King Barbecues	Lagostina®
Corelle®	Proctor Silex® Canada
Hamilton Beach® Canada	Tupperware®

Our special thanks to the following businesses for providing props for photography:

Anchor Hocking Canada	Pfaltzgraff Canada
Bernardin Ltd.	Pyrex® Storage
Canhome Global	Stokes
Corningware®	The Bay
Danesco Inc.	Totally Bamboo
Klass Works	Wal-Mart Canada Inc.
Michaels The Arts And Crafts Store	

Top: Birthday Loot Bags, page 162
Centre: Purse Bag, page 44
Bottom: Hot Chocolate Gift Package, page 160

Table of Contents

You'll find a little something special here for any occasion on the calendar—from the very first day of the New Year all the way through to Christmas.

For those special events that are just too important to miss— like birthdays, anniversaries, weddings or a new job—these homemade treats help you to mark the occasion in style!

When someone has gone the extra mile to lend a helping hand, these kitchen gifts will show them that all their hard work hasn't gone unnoticed.

Express your appreciation for the invite and reward the lucky hostess with some tasty treats that can be enjoyed after the event!

Show off your creative flair and save a little money too— these fancy favours give your guests a little something they can take home and savour long after the party's ended.

Sometimes words aren't enough to express just how much you care. These thoughtful kitchen gifts provide comfort to those facing tough times.

Kids can get in on the kitchen gifting action too! These special recipes and craft projects are built for the ultimate in kitchen fun—and make great gifts that the kids will be proud to give.

Find all your finishing touches right here—these craft ideas add gifting flair that elevates thoughtful gestures and delicious food into exciting gifts!

Foreword

It's the personal touches that make a gift special. When you know the recipient so well that you're sure you've got just the right gift, or when a thoughtful gesture brings a smile to a new friend's face, kitchen gifts are a great method for making someone's day a little bit brighter.

That's why we've created a helpful cookbook that's full of great recipes for gifting. But focusing on recipes alone didn't seem like quite enough—so we've included ideas for pulling the entire gift together, right down to the packaging that will hold the special treats you've made. Now, these are gifts that you've really put your heart into.

All-Occasion Gifts From Your Kitchen is loaded with terrific gift ideas to suit any occasion—there are great recipes for holidays, special events, parties and thank-you gifts. We've also added a special section of gifts meant to help your friends and neighbours through tough times, such as the loss of a family member, or busy times, such as the arrival of a new child. You'll find that each category of gift-giving has its own convenient section, so just jump to the section you're looking for and get gifting. Remember that you're not limited to our suggestions; you can modify the theme to suit any occasion you'd like. You're only limited by your own creativity when it comes to kitchen gifts!

Kitchen gifts are also a great way of getting the kids into the kitchen, so we've created a special section of fun recipes and craft projects just for them. But don't stop there—you can get your kids helping with all sorts of things, like measuring ingredients, stirring cookie dough, or even making crafty special touches for packaging your gifts. Kids love cooking and crafts, and kitchen gifting is an excellent way of encouraging them to get involved.

Of course all of the recipes in *All-Occasion Gifts From Your Kitchen* are also wonderful for any time. You can use this book as you would use any Company's Coming cookbook—it's full of great recipes that are sure to please your family as much as any other. Although this book may be full of gifting suggestions, we've made it easy for you to locate all your favourite recipes in our comprehensive index, so you're sure to find all the cookie recipes listed in one spot, and all the main dishes in another.

In addition to being full of great gifts you can put together yourself, *All-Occasion Gifts From Your Kitchen* makes an excellent gift for your friends and family. You could prepare a recipe and package it up with a copy of the book for your loved ones to use on their own. You may be lucky enough to receive some homemade goodies in return!

So, whether you're making a batch of Pink Lemonade Jellies for the hostess of a summer barbecue, or our I Love Ya Lasagna for a special friend who's lost someone near and dear, you'll find just the kitchen gift you're looking for in *All-Occasion Gifts From Your Kitchen*. It's a special gift—from our kitchen to yours.

Jean Paré

Nutrition Information Guidelines

Each recipe is analyzed using the most current version of the Canadian Nutrient File from Health Canada, which is based on the United States Department of Agriculture (USDA) Nutrient Database.

- If more than one ingredient is listed (such as "butter or hard margarine"), or if a range is given (1 – 2 tsp., 5 – 10 mL), only the first ingredient or first amount is analyzed.

- For meat, poultry and fish, the serving size per person is based on the recommended 4 oz. (113 g) uncooked weight (without bone), which is 2 – 3 oz. (57 – 85 g) cooked weight (without bone)—approximately the size of a deck of playing cards.

- Milk used is 1% M.F. (milk fat), unless otherwise stated.

- Cooking oil used is canola oil, unless otherwise stated.

- Ingredients indicating "sprinkle," "optional," or "for garnish" are not included in the nutrition information.

- The fat in recipes and combination foods can vary greatly depending on the sources and types of fats used in each specific ingredient. For these reasons, the amount of saturated, monounsaturated and polyunsaturated fats may not add up to the total fat content.

Vera C. Mazurak, Ph.D., Nutritionist

Tips for Easy Gift-Giving

Before You Begin

You never know when you're going to need to put together a small gift on short notice, so being prepared in advance really helps. If you keep some small kitchen gifts in the freezer for those last-minute invites, you'll never be left in the lurch. Dry mixes can also be made in advance and kept in a cool, dry place until a gifting occasion arises.

When it comes to wrapping up your gifts, the sky's the limit! You can personalize the wrapping to suit the recipient's personality or to match a particular theme. But the trick to making gift-wrapping a breeze is keeping a good supply of craft items on hand. We recommend keeping a selection of the following tools and craft supplies at the ready for convenient kitchen gifting:

Bows	Gift tags
Boxes	Glue gun
Cardboard	Hole punch
Cardstock	Jars and bottles
Cellophane bags and wrap	Needles and thread
Chenille stems	Pliers
Coloured pens	Ribbon
Cookie cutters	Scissors
Craft foam	Stamps and ink pads
Craft glue	Tape
Fabric remnants	Tissue paper
Felt	Wire cutters
Florist tape	Wrapping paper
Florist wire	

You can easily stock up on supplies as items go on sale. For example, you can buy remnant pieces of fabric from most fabric stores. These are just the small bits that are left at the end of a roll. Although they may not be large enough for a big sewing project, they work great for wrapping up a small package of sweets for a special friend, and they are often sold at a considerable discount!

Gift-Giving Etiquette

Not sure if it's appropriate to give a gift? Well, besides giving a thoughtful present just because you feel like it, there are times when it is just good manners to bring a little gift along.

When you've been invited to a dinner party, it's nice to bring a small hostess gift along with you. The hostess has put a lot of hard work into putting together a special dinner, and showing your appreciation goes a long way—and ensures future invites! Don't forget all those special people who go above and beyond the call of duty. Those teachers, caregivers, bus drivers or coaches deserve a big thank-you for all that they do.

There are also times when a thoughtful kitchen gift shows just how much you care. New parents, people who have just moved, or those facing difficult times can benefit greatly from a healthy, convenient meal or a comforting dessert. Instead of just sending flowers as a gesture of friendship, try sending some kitchen gifts.

Just because there may be a long distance between you and a loved one doesn't mean that you can't send a gift from your kitchen. Many of your homemade treats are great for sending through the mail. You'll want to select food items that won't spoil and are sturdy enough for mailing. Just wrap them up with care and send them on their way. Keep in mind that some food items, such as fruit and nuts, cannot be sent over international borders. Be sure to check each country's regulations before sending these types of foods into different countries.

The Finishing Touches

So you've got your kitchen gift prepared and it's wrapped and ready to go. Are you forgetting anything? Always remember to include any important information for reheating or preparing your kitchen gifts—don't assume that the recipient will always know the best method to use. We have included this information with each recipe; it can easily be photocopied and attached to the gift for easy reference.

You can always add special sentiments to the wrapping of your gift, or include a personalized tag to express an important message. Remember, it's the finishing touches that really pull a gift together. You can give someone a package of homemade treats anytime, but by making everything feel special and well thought out, you can turn your homemade cooking into a unique, personalized kitchen gift.

Calendar Occasions

They're those special events that happen once each year—holidays. From Valentine's Day to New Year's and all the occasions in between, these are the dates that you set aside every year for joyful celebrations. Give your usual Father's Day gift a unique spin, or perform a random act of kindness with a thoughtful, homemade gift.

Cinnamon Heart Cookies, right

Cinnamon Heart Cookies

This Valentine's Day, show everyone just how much you care with a giant heart-shaped cookie. The perfect small gift for a co-worker or a scrumptious alternative to paper valentines for your children's classmates.

CINNAMON COOKIES

All-purpose flour	3 cups	750 mL
Ground cinnamon	1 tbsp.	15 mL
Salt	1/2 tsp.	2 mL
Butter (or hard margarine), softened	1 cup	250 mL
Brown sugar, packed	1 cup	250 mL
Large eggs, fork-beaten	2	2
Vanilla extract	1 tsp.	5 mL

ROYAL ICING

Icing (confectioner's) sugar	7 1/3 cups	1.8 L
Water	1 cup	250 mL
Meringue (egg white) powder (see Note)	1/4 cup	60 mL
Red paste food colouring (see Tip, this page)	1/8 tsp.	0.5 mL
Red paste food colouring (see Tip, this page)	1/8 tsp.	0.5 mL

Cinnamon Cookies: Combine first 3 ingredients in medium bowl. Set aside.

Beat butter and brown sugar in large bowl until light and fluffy.

Add eggs and vanilla. Beat until smooth. Add flour mixture in 3 additions, beating well after each addition until no dry flour remains. Shape into flattened disc. Wrap with plastic wrap. Chill for at least 1 hour. Remove dough from refrigerator. Let stand for 10 minutes. Discard plastic wrap. Roll out dough on lightly floured surface to 1/4 inch (6 mm) thickness. Cut out shapes with lightly floured 5 inch (12.5 cm) heart-shaped cookie cutter. Roll out scraps to cut more heart shapes. Arrange cookies, about 1 inch (2.5 cm) apart, on greased cookie sheets. Bake, 1 sheet at a time, in 350°F (175°C) oven for about 12 minutes until golden. Let stand on cookie sheets for 5 minutes before removing to wire racks to cool. Cool cookie sheets between batches.

Royal Icing: Combine first 3 ingredients in large bowl. Add first amount of food colouring. Beat for about 8 minutes until soft peaks form. Spoon icing into piping bag fitted with small plain tip or small resealable freezer bag with tiny piece snipped off 1 corner. Pipe border around each cookie. Pipe icing to fill (see photo). Let stand overnight until set. Cover remaining icing with plastic wrap. Let stand at room temperature.

Add second amount of food colouring to remaining icing. Stir well. Spoon icing into same piping or freezer bag. Pipe decorative patterns on cookies. Makes about 12 cookies.

1 cookie: 622 Calories; 16.0 g Total Fat (4.0 g Mono, 0.6 g Poly, 9.9 g Sat); 76 mg Cholesterol; 114 g Carbohydrate; 1 g Fibre; 8 g Protein; 223 mg Sodium

Pictured at left and on page 11.

Note: Meringue powder is available at kitchen stores or cake decorating suppliers.

Orange-Spiced Honey

You won't have to ask anyone to "bee" your valentine if you're gifting this spicy-sweet honey. Makes a delicious glaze for roast pork or poultry, or combine with some butter for perfectly glazed squash or carrots.

Pasteurized liquid honey	1 cup	250 mL
Finely grated ginger root	1 tbsp.	15 mL
Grated orange zest	1 tbsp.	15 mL
Whole cloves	4	4

Combine all 4 ingredients in small saucepan. Bring to a boil on medium. Reduce heat to medium-low. Simmer, uncovered, for 5 minutes. Remove from heat. Let stand for 10 minutes. Strain through sieve into 2 cup (500 mL) liquid measure. Discard solids. Pour into 2 sterile 1/2 cup (125 mL) jars with tight-fitting lids. Store in refrigerator for up to 1 week. Makes about 1 cup (250 mL).

1 tbsp. (15 mL): 65 Calories; 0.0 g Total Fat (0.0 g Mono, 0.0 g Poly, 0.0 g Sat); 0 mg Cholesterol; 16 g Carbohydrate; trace Fibre; trace Protein; trace Sodium

Pictured on pages 11 and 157.

Tip: The advantage to using paste food colouring is that it allows for more vibrant colours than does liquid food colouring. If you try to substitute liquid food colouring for paste food colouring, the addition of the additional liquid may affect the success of the recipe.

Zesty Zinfandel Jelly

Wine adds a touch of class to this spicy jelly, and makes it the perfect addition to a gift basket packed with gourmet goodies. Serve with cheese, crackers and fruit, or as a condiment with roasted meats.

White Zinfandel (or rosé) wine	2 cups	500 mL
Finely chopped red pepper	1/2 cup	125 mL
Lemon juice	1/3 cup	75 mL
Dried crushed chilies	1 tsp.	5 mL
Grated lemon zest	1 tsp.	5 mL
Box of pectin crystals	2 oz.	57 g
Granulated sugar	4 cups	1 L

Combine first 5 ingredients in Dutch oven.

Add pectin. Heat and stir on high for about 4 minutes until mixture begins to boil.

Add sugar. Heat and stir for about 3 minutes until mixture comes to a hard boil. Boil for 2 minutes, stirring constantly. Remove from heat. Stir for 5 minutes to suspend chilies. Fill 8 hot sterile 1/2 cup (125 mL) jars to within 1/4 inch (6 mm) of top. Wipe rims. Place sterile metal lids on jars and screw on metal bands fingertip tight. Do not over-tighten. Process in boiling water bath for 10 minutes (see Note). Remove jars. Let stand at room temperature until cool. Chill after opening. Makes about 4 cups (1 L).

1 tbsp. (15 mL): 53 Calories; trace Total Fat (0 g Mono, 0 g Poly, 0 g Sat); 0 mg Cholesterol; 12 g Carbohydrate; trace Fibre; trace Protein; trace Sodium

Note: Processing time is for elevations 1001 to 3000 feet (306 to 915 m) above sea level. Make adjustment for elevation in your area if necessary.

Sesame Nut Crunch

Show your valentine that you've gone nuts for them with this candy-coated mix. You can package this crunchy combination in small cellophane bags for all your loved ones, or put it all in a large decorative jar or tin for that one special someone.

Brown sugar, packed	1 cup	250 mL
Water	1/4 cup	60 mL
Corn syrup	1 tbsp.	15 mL
Salt	1/4 tsp.	1 mL
Pecan halves (see Note)	1 cup	250 mL
Unsalted, roasted cashews	1 cup	250 mL
Whole blanched almonds (see Note)	1 cup	250 mL
Sesame seeds, toasted (see Tip, page 41), see Note	1/4 cup	60 mL

Combine first 4 ingredients in large saucepan. Bring to a boil on medium, stirring often until sugar is dissolved. Boil for about 8 minutes until mixture reaches soft ball stage (about 240°F, 116°C) on candy thermometer (see Tip, page 77) or until small amount dropped into very cold water forms a soft ball that flattens on its own accord when removed. Remove from heat.

Add remaining 4 ingredients. Stir well. Spread evenly in greased baking sheet with sides. Cool. Break into pieces. Makes about 6 cups (1.5 L).

1/4 cup (60 mL): 141 Calories; 9.2 g Total Fat (3.3 g Mono, 1.4 g Poly, 0.8 g Sat); 0 mg Cholesterol; 13 g Carbohydrate; 1 g Fibre; 3 g Protein; 29 mg Sodium

Pictured at right.

Note: You can pick your favourite nuts to mix together. A wide variety of nuts, including sesame seeds, is available in the bulk section of the grocery store.

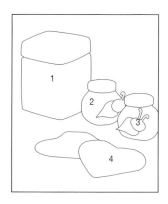

1. Sesame Nut Crunch, above
2. Orange-Spiced Honey, page 9
3. Bee Mine Tag, page 157
4. Cinnamon Heart Cookies, page 9

Truffle Kisses

These deep, rich chocolate truffles are made extra-special with a kiss of coffee and cinnamon flavour. Package your truffles in a Chocolate Box, at right, for a truly unique and special presentation. You're sure to receive kisses of gratitude in return for your generosity!

Dark chocolate bars, chopped (3 1/2 oz.,100 g, each)	2	2
Whipping cream	1/4 cup	60 mL
Ground cinnamon	1 tsp.	5 mL
Instant coffee granules	1 tsp.	5 mL
Dark chocolate melting wafers	1 cup	250 mL
Red candy melting wafers	2 tbsp.	30 mL
White candy melting wafers	2 tbsp.	30 mL

Heat first 4 ingredients in small heavy saucepan on lowest heat, stirring often, until chocolate is almost melted. Remove from heat. Stir until smooth. Chill for about 2 1/2 hours until firm. Roll into 1 inch (2.5 cm) balls. Arrange on waxed paper-lined baking sheet. Chill for about 20 minutes until set.

Put chocolate wafers into small microwave-safe cup (see Tip, below). Microwave on medium (50%), stirring every 30 seconds, until almost melted. Stir until smooth. Place 1 ball on end of wooden pick. Dip ball into chocolate, allowing excess to drip back into cup. Place on same waxed paper-lined baking sheet. Repeat with remaining balls and chocolate. Chill until set.

Put red and white melting wafers into separate small microwave-safe cups. Microwave, uncovered, on medium (50%), stirring every 15 seconds, until almost melted. Stir until smooth. Spoon into separate piping bags fitted with smallest tips. Pipe decorative pattern over each ball (see Tip, page 154). Makes about 26 truffles.

1 truffle: 90 Calories; 5.9 g Total Fat (0.5 g Mono, 0.1 g Poly, 3.6 g Sat); 4 mg Cholesterol; 10 g Carbohydrate; 1 g Fibre; 1 g Protein; 5 mg Sodium

Pictured at right.

Tip: Use a deep container (a glass measuring cup or a tall narrow saucepan works well) to hold melted chocolate or melting wafers. The chocolate will stay warm longer and will coat better.

How To

Chocolate Box

What to pack into a box made entirely of chocolate? More chocolate!

Dark chocolate melting wafers	2 cups	500 mL
Red candy melting wafers	2 tbsp.	30 mL
White candy melting wafers	2 tbsp.	30 mL

Invert 2 large baking sheets on work surface. Cover with parchment (not waxed) paper. Set aside. Put chocolate wafers into medium microwave-safe bowl. Microwave, uncovered, on medium (50%), stirring every 30 seconds, until almost melted. Stir until smooth. Reserve 2 tbsp. (30 mL) in small cup. Keep warm. Spread remaining chocolate evenly on prepared baking sheets to 1/8 inch (3 mm) thickness. Chill for about 3 minutes until set. Lay clean ruler on 1 chocolate sheet. Use a sharp knife to cut straight edges to make two 5 x 5 inch (12.5 x 12.5 cm) squares for base and top. Lay clean ruler on second chocolate sheet. Use a sharp knife to cut straight edges to make four 4 7/8 x 2 inch (12.5 x 5 cm) rectangles for sides. Melt scraps to create decorations for top of box.

Put red and white candy melting wafers into separate microwave-safe cups. Microwave on medium (50%), stirring every 15 seconds, until almost melted. Stir until smooth. Spoon into separate piping bags fitted with smallest tips. Pipe decorative shapes on top and sides of chocolate box (see Tip, page 154). Attach sides to base, 1 at a time, using reserved chocolate and paintbrush (see photo). Attach decorations to top with remaining chocolate. Chill until set. Makes 1 box.

1 box: 2440 Calories; 155.3 g Total Fat (5.4 g Mono, 0.6 g Poly, 87.2 g Sat); 8 mg Cholesterol; 308 g Carbohydrate; 30 g Fibre; 34 g Protein; 205 mg Sodium

Pictured at right.

Chocolate Box, above, with Truffle Kisses, this page

Tangy Carrot Marmalade

This pretty, orange marmalade comes with a twist. Sweet carrots with a little heat from ginger and cinnamon add an element of surprise to this old favourite. Make it the perfect gift with Hot Cross Muffin Mix, page 15.

Medium oranges (see Tip, page 15)	2	2
Medium lemon (see Tip, page 15)	1	1
Grated carrot	1 cup	250 mL
Julienned ginger root (see Note 1)	3 tbsp.	50 mL
Baking soda	1/8 tsp.	0.5 mL
Cinnamon sticks (4 inches, 10 cm, each)	4	4
Water	3 1/4 cups	800 mL
Box of pectin crystals	2 oz.	57 g
Granulated sugar	5 cups	1.3 L

Remove rind from oranges and lemon using vegetable peeler. Cut into 1/8 x 1 inch (0.3 x 2.5 cm) strips. Combine rind and next 3 ingredients in Dutch oven. Place 12 inch (30 cm) square of double-layered cheesecloth in medium bowl. Cut oranges and lemon into quarters. Squeeze juice into cheesecloth-lined bowl.

Place juiced fruit pieces and cinnamon sticks in centre of cheesecloth square. Draw up corners and tie with butcher's string. Add cheesecloth bag and juice to pot. Add water. Bring to a boil. Reduce heat to medium. Boil gently, uncovered, for about 25 minutes, stirring occasionally, until zest is softened. Transfer cheesecloth bag to medium bowl. Let stand until cool enough to handle. Squeeze liquid from cheesecloth bag into carrot mixture. Discard bag. Stir. Makes about 3 cups (750 mL) carrot mixture. If less, add water to make 3 cups (750 mL).

Add pectin. Heat and stir on high for about 3 minutes until mixture begins to boil.

(continued on next page)

Spiced Carrot Antipasto

Easter isn't just about chocolate and Easter eggs—this unique antipasto is packed with roasted vegetables, dried apricots and exotic spices for a truly grown-up Easter gift. Great served with pita chips, apple slices or crackers.

Medium carrots, halved lengthwise and cut into 1/4 inch (6 mm) slices	8	8
Medium parsnip, halved lengthwise and cut into 1/4 inch (6 mm) slices	1	1
Small red onion, cut into 1/4 inch (6 mm) slices	1	1
Olive (or cooking) oil	1 1/2 tbsp.	25 mL
Chopped dried apricot	1 cup	250 mL
Dry (or alcohol-free) white wine	1/2 cup	125 mL
Can of diced tomatoes (with juice)	14 oz.	398 mL
Ketchup	1 1/2 cups	375 mL
Chopped large pitted green olives	1/2 cup	125 mL
Chopped pitted kalamata olives	1/2 cup	125 mL
Ground cinnamon	1 1/2 tsp.	7 mL
Ground cumin	1 1/2 tsp.	7 mL
Chili paste (sambal oelek)	1/2 tsp.	2 mL

Put first 3 ingredients into medium bowl. Add olive oil. Toss well. Spread evenly on large greased baking sheet. Toss with olive oil. Bake in 375°F (190°C) oven for about 50 minutes, turning at halftime, until vegetables are soft and lightly browned. Cool. Chop finely. Set aside.

Combine apricot and wine in large saucepan. Bring to a boil. Remove from heat. Let stand for 15 minutes.

Add remaining 7 ingredients and vegetables. Cook on medium for about 10 minutes, stirring often, until mixture comes to a boil. Fill 6 hot sterile 1 cup (250 mL) jars with tight-fitting lids. Store in refrigerator for up to 1 week or freeze in an airtight container for up to 1 month. Makes about 5 1/2 cups (1.4 L).

1 tbsp. (15 mL): 22 Calories; 0.7 g Total Fat (0.3 g Mono, 0.1 g Poly, trace Sat); 0 mg Cholesterol; 4 g Carbohydrate; trace Fibre; trace Protein; 80 mg Sodium

Pictured on page 16.

Add sugar. Heat and stir until mixture comes to a hard boil. Boil for 1 minute, stirring occasionally. Remove from heat. Stir for 5 minutes to suspend fruit. Fill 5 hot sterile 1 cup (250 mL) jars to within 1/4 inch (6 mm) of top. Wipe rims. Place sterile metal lids on jars and screw on metal bands fingertip tight. Do not over-tighten. Process in boiling water bath for 10 minutes (see Note 2). Remove jars. Let stand at room temperature until cool. Refrigerate after opening. Makes about 5 cups (1.25 L).

1 tbsp. (15 mL): 49 Calories; trace Total Fat (0 g Mono, 0 g Poly, 0 g Sat); 0 mg Cholesterol; 13 g Carbohydrate; trace Fibre; trace Protein; 3 mg Sodium

Pictured on page 16.

Note 1: To julienne, cut into very thin strips that resemble matchsticks.

Note 2: Processing time is for elevations 1001 to 3000 feet (306 to 915 m) above sea level. Make adjustment for elevation in your area if necessary.

Hot Cross Muffin Mix

Hot cross muffins are an Easter morning favourite. This convenient mix makes baking up a batch of hot muffins hassle-free. A disposable piping bag of icing sugar completes this truly thoughtful Easter treat. Perfect with a jar of Tangy Carrot Marmalade, page 14.

Brown sugar, packed	3/4 cup	175 mL
All-purpose flour	1 cup	250 mL
Buttermilk powder	1/4 cup	60 mL
Salt	1/2 tsp.	2 mL
All-purpose flour	1 cup	250 mL
Baking powder	1 tbsp.	15 mL
Ground cinnamon	1 tsp.	5 mL
Ground nutmeg	1/4 tsp.	1 mL
Ground cardamom	1/8 tsp.	0.5 mL
Ground cloves, just a pinch		
Chopped glazed pineapple	3/4 cup	175 mL
Currants (or dark raisins)	1/2 cup	125 mL
Icing (confectioner's) sugar	1 cup	250 mL

Pack brown sugar evenly in bottom of jar with tight-fitting lid.

Combine next 3 ingredients in medium bowl. Spoon over brown sugar.

Combine next 6 ingredients in same medium bowl. Spoon over flour mixture.

Combine pineapple and currants in small resealable or decorative plastic bag. Place on top of flour mixture. Makes about 4 cups (1 L).

Measure icing sugar into disposable piping bag and attach to jar.

Pictured on page 16.

Directions for Hot Cross Muffins:

Remove bag of fruit from jar. Set aside. Empty contents of jar into large bowl. Stir. Make a well in centre. Whisk 1 large egg, 1/4 cup (60 mL) cooking oil and 1 cup (250 mL) water in small bowl. Add to well. Add fruit mixture. Stir until just moistened. Fill 12 greased muffin cups 3/4 full. Bake in 375°F (190°C) oven for about 20 minutes until wooden pick inserted in centre of muffin comes out clean. Let stand in pan for 5 minutes before removing to wire rack to cool.

Directions for Icing:

Empty contents of piping bag into small bowl. Add 4 tsp. (20 mL) water. Stir until smooth. Spoon icing into same piping bag. Snip tiny piece off bottom. Pipe crosses onto muffins. Makes 12 muffins.

1 muffin: 265 Calories; 5.3 g Total Fat (2.7 g Mono, 1.4 g Poly, 0.6 g Sat); 20 mg Cholesterol; 53 g Carbohydrate; 1 g Fibre; 3 g Protein; 273 mg Sodium

Tip: When using large amounts of citrus zest, choose fruits with thick, waxy skins. They usually have the best oil content. The deeper the colour, the more colour the finished product will have. Scrub fruits with a vegetable brush under hot water to remove any pesticide or wax residues before zesting.

How To

Easter Chick Box

Easter baskets are so passé! Package up your Easter goodies in a pretty homemade box for a modernized approach.

MATERIALS
Orange craft foam (1/16 inch, 1.5 mm, thick)
Yellow craft foam (1/16 inch, 1.5 mm, thick)
Purple craft foam (1/16 inch, 1.5 mm, thick)
2 orange chenille stems (1/8 inch, 3 mm, thick)
4 yellow feathers
7 inch (18 cm) square box
Package of flower and stem craft foam pieces
Excelsior (optional)

TOOLS
scissors, pencil, fine-point black pen (non-bleed), fast-grab tacky glue, wire cutters, low-temperature glue gun, needle-nosed pliers

Enlarge patterns by 200%. Cut out each piece. Using a pencil, trace the enlarged pattern pieces onto the coloured craft foam as follows:

Orange: 1 beak (Pattern 1), 2 feet (Pattern 2), and 2 very small triangles (no pattern) for baby chick beaks

Yellow: 1 momma chick (Pattern 3) and 2 baby chicks (Pattern 4)

Purple: 1 hat (Pattern 5) with small slit for head

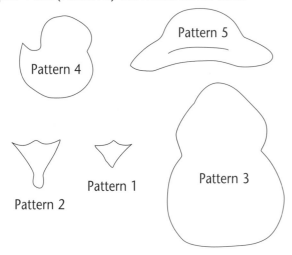

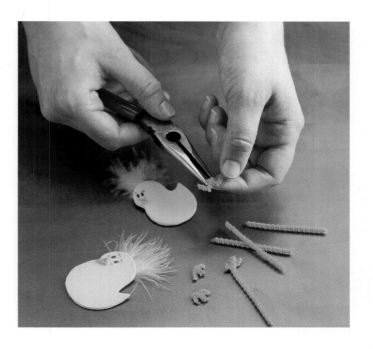

Glue the hat to the momma chick's body with tacky glue. Draw 2 small lines on beak for nostrils. Centre the beak on face and glue in place. Let dry. Draw the eyes and other details. To make legs, cut a 4 inch (10 cm) length of chenille stem with wire cutters. Poke one end of stem through foot where leg would be.

Secure the foot by bending the end of the stem under the foot. Repeat with the other end of the stem and foot. Fold the stem in half. Glue with glue gun to the back of the momma chick's body.

Using tacky glue, attach feathers to the heads and tails of baby chicks. Draw the eyes and other details. Centre the beaks on baby chick faces and glue in place. Let dry. Cut chenille stem into four 1 inch (2.5 cm) pieces and four 2 inch (5 cm) pieces. To make a foot, take one 1 inch (2.5 cm) length of stem and form into a small 'w' shape. With the needle-nosed pliers, press the middle of the 'w' together so it looks like 3 toes (see photo).

Repeat with remaining 1 inch (2.5 cm) pieces. Place a dab of hot glue on 1 end of each 2 inch (5 cm) length of chenille stem and attach to feet. Let dry. Glue 2 legs on each chick using the glue gun.

Decorate the hat as desired with flower and stem foam, using tacky glue. Glue all the chicks onto the box using the glue gun. Use the rest of your flowers and stems to decorate the remaining sides of the box as desired. Fill the box with excelsior.

Pictured at left.

1. Hot Cross Muffin Mix, page 15
2. Spiced Carrot Antipasto, page 14,
3. Easter Chick Box, above
4. Tangy Carrot Marmalade, page 14

Bouquet of Cookie Flowers

Give the gift of flowers with a unique twist—they're completely edible! Sure to bring a smile to the lucky recipient's face, and the perfect way to show your appreciation. A great choice for Administrative Professional's Day or a spring-themed gift.

All-purpose flour	1 1/2 cups	375 mL
Baking powder	1 1/2 tsp.	7 mL
Ground cardamom	1/4 tsp.	1 mL
Ground cinnamon	1/4 tsp.	1 mL
Ground nutmeg	1/4 tsp.	1 mL
Salt	1/4 tsp.	1 mL
Butter (or hard margarine), softened	1/2 cup	125 mL
Granulated sugar	1/2 cup	125 mL
Large egg	1	1
Vanilla extract	1/2 tsp.	2 mL
Drops of red liquid food colouring	8	8
Drops of yellow liquid food colouring	8	8
Lollipop sticks (5 inches, 12.5 cm, each)	16	16
Candy-coated chocolate candies	16	16

Combine first 6 ingredients in small bowl. Set aside.

Beat butter and sugar in large bowl until light and fluffy. Add egg and vanilla. Beat until smooth. Add flour mixture in 2 additions, mixing well after each addition until no dry flour remains. Divide dough into 2 equal portions.

Add red food colouring to 1 dough portion. Knead in bowl until colour is even. Shape into disc. Wrap with plastic wrap. Chill for at least 1 hour. Repeat with remaining dough and yellow food colouring. Discard plastic wrap from pink dough. Roll out between 2 sheets of waxed paper to 1/4 inch (6 mm) thickness. Discard top sheet of waxed paper. Cut out shapes with lightly floured 2 1/2 inch (6.4 cm) flower-shaped cookie cutters. Roll out scraps to cut more flower shapes.

Insert 1 lollipop stick into side of 1 flower shape. Place on greased cookie sheet. Press one chocolate candy into centre of flower shape. Repeat with remaining flower shapes, lollipop sticks and chocolate candies. Arrange, about 1 inch (2.5 cm) apart, on cookie sheet, alternating direction of sticks. Bake in 350°F (175°C) oven for about 10 minutes until edges are golden. Let stand on cookie sheets for 5 minutes before removing to wire rack to cool completely. Cool cookie sheet between batches. Repeat with yellow dough. Makes about 16 cookies.

1 cookie: 95 Calories; 3.2 g Total Fat (0.9 g Mono, 0.2 g Poly, 2.0 g Sat); 21 mg Cholesterol; 15 g Carbohydrate; trace Fibre; 2 g Protein; 112 mg Sodium

Pictured at right.

Trail Mix Royale

Looking for the perfect way to show how much you appreciate that special administrative assistant who always keeps things in order at work? Pack this handy trail mix in a decorative container that can be easily tucked into a desk drawer for mid-morning snack attacks.

Dried apricots, quartered	1 cup	250 mL
Dried cherries, halved	1 cup	250 mL
Pistachios, toasted (see Tip, page 41)	1 cup	250 mL
Salted cashews	1 cup	250 mL
Whole natural almonds, toasted (see Tip, page 34)	1 cup	250 mL
Yogurt-covered raisins	1 cup	250 mL

Combine all 6 ingredients in large bowl. Makes about 6 cups (1.5 L).

1/4 cup (60 mL): 165 Calories; 9.3 g Total Fat (1.3 g Mono, 0.7 g Poly, 1.7 g Sat); trace Cholesterol; 17 g Carbohydrate; 3 g Fibre; 4 g Protein; 49 mg Sodium

Pictured at right.

Clockwise from Left:
File Folder Card, page 163
Bouquet Of Cookie Flowers, above, with Picket Fence Box, at right
Trail Mix Royale, above

How To

Picket Fence Box

*Spring is in the air! Give the gift of edible flowers
planted in a cute little fenced-in garden.*

MATERIALS
Acrylic craft paint (any colour)
4 x 4 x 2 1/2 inch (10 x 10 x 6.4 cm) paper mâché box
4 fence pieces (4 inches, 10 cm, long)
16 pieces of coloured ribbon (1/8 inch, 3 mm, width),
  5 inches (12.5 cm) long
Dry florist foam (4 x 4 x 2 inch, 10 x 10 x 5 cm, piece)
Iridescent excelsior
Bouquet of Cookie Flowers, at left

TOOLS
paint brush, glue gun, scissors

Paint the box and fence. Let dry. Glue the ends of the ribbon
pieces to the wrong side of the fence pieces, at the ends of
the horizontal slats of wood. Let dry.

Glue 1 fence piece to the centre of each side of the box.
Tie each ribbon into a bow with a ribbon from the adjacent
fence piece. Trim the loose ribbon ends.

Secure the florist foam inside the box with hot glue. Place
tissue over foam to cover, tucking in edges to hide. Poke
stems of cookie flowers through the tissue into the foam.

Pictured below.

Earl-y Morning Spiced Tea Blend

Make Mom's first cup of morning tea a memorable one with this blend of aromatic spices and classic Earl Grey.

Whole loose Earl Grey tea	1/4 cup	60 mL
Whole cloves	48	48
Whole green cardamom, bruised	18	18
(see Tip, page 120)		
Cinnamon sticks	6	6
(4 inches, 10 cm, each)		

Arrange six 6 inch (15 cm) squares of double-layered cheesecloth on work surface. Put 2 tsp. (10 mL) tea leaves, 8 whole cloves and 3 cardamom pods into centre of each cheesecloth square. Break 1 cinnamon stick into pieces. Add to tea mixture. Draw up corners and tie with butcher's string. Repeat with remaining cheesecloth squares, tea, cloves, cardamom and cinnamon. Makes 6 spiced tea pouches.

Pictured on page 23.

Directions for Earl-y Morning Spiced Tea:

Put 1 tea pouch into preheated teapot. Pour 2 cups (500 mL) boiling water over pouch. Let steep for about 10 minutes. Squeeze and discard tea pouch. Makes about 2 cups (500 mL).

1 cup (250 mL) tea: 0 Calories; 0.0 g Total Fat (0.0 g Mono, 0.0 g Poly, 0.0 g Sat); 0 mg Cholesterol; 0 g Carbohydrate; 0 g Fibre; 0 g Protein; 0 mg Sodium

---

Sweet Mama Sugar Scrub

Mom always goes the extra mile when it comes to her kids, so give her tired hands a break with this gentle exfoliating scrub that will leave her skin feeling soft and refreshed. Personalize the gift by using your mom's favourite scent in place of lavender.

Granulated sugar	2/3 cup	150 mL
Lavender-scented liquid dish soap	1/4 cup	60 mL

Combine sugar and soap in small bowl. Transfer to decorative jar with tight-fitting lid. Store in cool dry place for up to 4 months. Makes about 3/4 cup (175 mL).

Pictured at right.

Directions for Sweet Mama Sugar Scrub:

Rub a small amount on wet skin. Rinse well.

Hazelnut Truffles

Decadent truffles are a sure-fire way to show how much you care. Let Mom know how much you appreciate all that she does by giving her a box of these melt-in-your-mouth homemade chocolates, packed with hazelnuts and toffee crunch. And she'll never know if you save a couple for yourself—they're just too good to pass up!

Dark chocolate bar, chopped	3 1/2 oz.	100 g
Whipping cream	1/4 cup	60 mL
Chocolate hazelnut spread	1/2 cup	125 mL
Toffee bits (such as Skor)	1/2 cup	125 mL
Chocolate melting wafers	1 1/2 cups	375 mL
Finely chopped sliced hazelnuts	1 cup	250 mL
(filberts), toasted (see Tip, page 41)		

Heat chocolate and cream in small heavy saucepan on lowest heat, stirring often, until chocolate is almost melted. Remove from heat. Stir until smooth.

Add chocolate hazelnut spread. Stir until smooth. Add toffee bits. Stir. Let stand at room temperature for about 2 hours until firm. Roll into balls, using about 2 tsp. (10 mL) for each. Arrange on waxed paper-lined baking sheet. Chill for about 20 minutes until set.

Heat chocolate wafers in small heavy saucepan on lowest heat, stirring often, until almost melted. Remove from heat. Stir until smooth. Transfer to small cup (see Tip, page 12). Put hazelnuts into shallow dish. Place 1 ball on end of wooden pick. Dip ball into chocolate until completely coated, allowing excess to drip back into cup. Roll in hazelnuts until coated. Place on same waxed paper-lined baking sheet. Remove wooden pick. Repeat with remaining balls, chocolate and nuts (see Tip, page 154). Chill until set. Makes about 26 truffles.

1 truffle: 135 Calories; 9.3 g Total Fat (3.3 g Mono, 0.7 g Poly, 4.0 g Sat); 6 mg Cholesterol; 13 g Carbohydrate; 1 g Fibre; 1 g Protein; 22 mg Sodium

Pictured at right.

Left: Sweet Mama Sugar Scrub, this page
Right: Hazelnut Truffles, above

Ruby Marmalade

If Mom is the queen of homemade preserves, show her that she's not the only one who has mastered the skill! This rosy-pink marmalade is full of citrusy goodness with a special touch from cherries and a Scottish liqueur.

Large red grapefruit (see Tip, page 15)	1	1
Large orange (see Tip, page 15)	1	1
Large lemon (see Tip, page 15)	1	1
Baking soda	1/8 tsp.	0.5 mL
Red glazed cherries, chopped	1/2 cup	125 mL
Water	3 cups	750 mL
Box of pectin crystals	2 oz.	57 g
Granulated sugar	5 cups	1.25 L
Red glazed cherries, finely chopped	1/2 cup	125 mL
Drambuie	1/4 cup	60 mL

Remove rind from grapefruit, orange and lemon using vegetable peeler. Cut into 1/8 x 1 inch (0.3 x 2.5 cm) strips. Put into Dutch oven. Sprinkle with baking soda. Lay 12 inch (30 cm) square of double-layered cheesecloth in medium bowl. Cut grapefruit, orange and lemon into quarters. Squeeze juice into cheesecloth-lined bowl.

Place juiced fruit pieces and first amount of cherries in centre of cheesecloth square. Draw up corners and tie with butcher's string. Add cheesecloth bag and juice to pot. Add water. Stir. Bring to a boil. Reduce heat to medium. Boil gently, uncovered, for about 30 minutes, stirring occasionally, until rind is softened. Transfer cheesecloth bag to medium bowl. Let stand until cool enough to handle. Squeeze liquid from cheesecloth bag into rind mixture. Discard bag. Stir. Makes about 3 cups (750 mL). If less, add water to make 3 cups (750 mL).

Add pectin. Heat and stir on high for about 2 minutes until mixture begins to boil.

Add sugar. Heat and stir for about 3 minutes until mixture comes to a hard boil. Boil for 1 minute, stirring occasionally. Remove from heat.

Add second amount of cherries and liqueur. Stir for 5 minutes to suspend fruit. Fill 5 hot sterile 1 cup (250 mL) jars to within 1/4 inch (6 mm) of top. Wipe rims. Place sterile metal lids on jars and screw on metal bands fingertip tight. Do not over-tighten. Process in boiling water bath for 10 minutes (see Note). Remove jars. Let stand at room temperature until cool. Chill after opening. Makes about 5 cups (1.25 L).

1 tbsp. (15 mL): 56 Calories; trace Total Fat (0 g Mono, 0 g Poly, 0 g Sat); 0 mg Cholesterol; 14 g Carbohydrate; trace Fibre; trace Protein; 2.3 mg Sodium

Pictured at right.

Note: Processing time is for elevations 1001 to 3000 feet (306 to 915 m) above sea level. Make adjustment for elevation in your area if necessary.

Orange Vanilla Scones

Give Mom a gift that's been inspired by a few tea-time favourites from the United Kingdom. Package up these tender scones with a jar of Ruby Marmalade, at left, and Earl-y Morning Spiced Tea Blend, page 20.

All-purpose flour	2 1/4 cups	550 mL
Granulated sugar	1/4 cup	60 mL
Baking powder	2 tsp.	10 mL
Baking soda	1/2 tsp.	2 mL
Salt	1/2 tsp.	2 mL
Cold butter (or hard margarine), cut up	1/3 cup	75 mL
Large egg, fork-beaten	1	1
Plain yogurt	1/3 cup	75 mL
Orange juice	1/4 cup	60 mL
Grated orange zest (see Tip, page 118)	1 tbsp.	15 mL
Vanilla extract	1 1/2 tsp.	7 mL
Milk	1 tbsp.	15 mL
Granulated sugar	1 tbsp.	15 mL

Combine first 5 ingredients in large bowl. Cut in butter until mixture resembles coarse crumbs. Make a well in centre.

Combine next 5 ingredients in small bowl. Add to well. Stir until soft dough forms. Turn out onto lightly floured surface. Knead 6 times. Roll or pat out to 3/4 inch (2 cm) thickness. Cut out shapes with lightly floured 2 inch (5 cm) flower-shaped cookie cutter. Roll out scraps to cut more flower shapes.

Brush with milk. Sprinkle with second amount of sugar. Arrange, about 1 inch (2.5 cm) apart, on greased baking sheet. Bake in 400°F (205°C) oven for about 12 minutes until golden. Let stand on baking sheet for 5 minutes before removing to wire rack to cool. Makes about 24 biscuits.

1 biscuit: 78 Calories; 2.7 g Total Fat (0.7 g Mono, 0.1 g Poly, 1.7 g Sat); 16 mg Cholesterol; 12 g Carbohydrate; trace Fibre; 2 g Protein; 145 mg Sodium

Pictured at right.

Clockwise from Left:
Orange Vanilla Scones, above
Ruby Marmalade, this page
Earl-y Morning Spiced Tea Blend, page 20
Photo Flip Card, page 163

Bourbon Bow Tie Cookies

Let Dad enjoy one of his favourite spirits in a dark and delicious chocolate cookie with a special bourbon-flavoured filling. Decorate to suit his unique personality for a tie that he will be truly happy to receive!

CHOCOLATE CINNAMON COOKIES

Large egg	1	1
Egg yolk (large)	1	1
Instant coffee granules	1 tbsp.	15 mL
Vanilla extract	2 tsp.	10 mL
All-purpose flour	2 1/2 cups	625 mL
Cocoa, sifted if lumpy	1 cup	250 mL
Ground cinnamon	2 tsp.	10 mL
Salt	1/2 tsp.	2 mL
Butter (or hard margarine), softened	1 cup	250 mL
Granulated sugar	1 cup	250 mL

ROYAL ICING

Icing (confectioner's) sugar	2 cups	500 mL
Egg white, large	1	1
Water	1/4 cup	60 mL
Liquid food colourings		
Assorted sprinkles (optional)		

BOURBON BUTTER FROSTING

Icing (confectioner's) sugar	2 cups	500 mL
Butter (or hard margarine), softened	1/2 cup	125 mL
Bourbon whiskey	2 tbsp.	30 mL

Chocolate Cinnamon Cookies: Whisk first 4 ingredients in small bowl. Let stand for 5 minutes.

Combine next 4 ingredients in medium bowl.

Beat butter and sugar in large bowl until light and fluffy. Add egg mixture. Beat until smooth. Add flour mixture in 2 additions, beating well after each addition until no dry flour remains. Shape into flattened square. Roll out dough on lightly floured surface to 11 x 14 inch (28 x 35 cm) rectangle. Cut into shapes using lightly floured 4 inch (10 cm) bow tie-shaped cookie cutter. Roll out scraps to cut more shapes. Arrange cookies, about 1 inch (2.5 cm) apart, on greased cookie sheets. Bake in 350°F (175°C) oven for about 10 minutes until firm. Let stand on cookie sheets for 5 minutes before removing to wire racks to cool. Cool cookie sheets between batches. Makes about 32 cookies.

Royal Icing: Combine first 3 ingredients in large bowl. Beat for about 10 minutes until smooth. Makes about 1 1/2 cups (375 mL) icing.

Divide icing into separate small bowls. Colour with food colourings as desired. Spoon icing into piping bags fitted with small plain tips or small resealable freezer bags with tiny piece snipped off 1 corner. Decorate half of cookies with icing and sprinkles. Let stand for at least 8 hours or overnight until set.

Bourbon Butter Frosting: Combine all 3 ingredients in medium bowl. Beat for about 3 minutes until light and fluffy. Makes about 1 1/3 cups (325 mL) frosting. Spread about 1 tbsp. (15 mL) on bottom of undecorated cookies. Place decorated cookies, icing-side up, over frosting. Makes 16 sandwich cookies.

1 cookie: 414 Calories; 18.1 g Total Fat (4.6 g Mono, 0.7 g Poly, 11.0 g Sat); 71 mg Cholesterol; 60 g Carbohydrate; 1 g Fibre; 4 g Protein; 202 mg Sodium

Pictured at right.

Round-The-World Barbecue Blast

This barbecue sauce combines the world's greatest flavours for the world's greatest dad. A blend of ethnic seasonings comes together to create the perfect topping for grilled pork, poultry or beef.

Balsamic vinegar	2 tbsp.	30 mL
Brown sugar, packed	2 tbsp.	30 mL
Tandoori curry paste	2 tbsp.	30 mL
Chinese five-spice powder	1 tbsp.	15 mL
Minced onion flakes	1 tbsp.	15 mL
Paprika	1 tbsp.	15 mL
Garlic powder	2 tsp.	10 mL
Salt	1 tsp.	5 mL
Pepper	1/2 tsp.	2 mL
Cayenne pepper	1/4 tsp.	1 mL

Combine all 10 ingredients in small bowl. Spoon into jar with tight-fitting lid. Store in refrigerator for up to 3 weeks. Makes about 1/2 cup (125 mL).

Pictured at right.

Directions for Round-The-World Barbecue Blast:

Brush onto beef, pork or poultry. Let stand in refrigerator for at least 30 minutes or up to 4 hours before cooking.

1 tsp. (5 mL) rub: 9.3 Calories; 0.1 g Total Fat (0 g Mono, trace Poly, trace Sat); 0 mg Cholesterol; 2 g Carbohydrate; trace Fibre; trace Protein; 126 mg Sodium

---

Superhero Beef Jerky

Show Dad that he's still your hero! This peppery beef jerky is balanced nicely with a little maple sweetness. You could omit the cayenne pepper for a milder jerky.

Maple (or maple-flavoured) syrup	1/2 cup	125 mL
Soy sauce	1/4 cup	60 mL
Ground ginger	4 tsp.	20 mL
Garlic powder	1 tsp.	5 mL
Salt	2 tsp.	10 mL
Cayenne pepper	1/2 tsp.	2 mL
Beef eye of round roast, cut in half lengthwise	2 lbs.	900 g

Combine first 6 ingredients in extra-large resealable freezer bag.

Cut beef diagonally across the grain into 1/8 inch (3 mm) slices (see Note). Add to maple mixture. Seal bag. Turn until coated. Let stand in refrigerator for at least 8 hours or overnight. Set wire racks in 2 large foil-lined baking sheets with sides. Draw beef slices across edge of freezer bag to remove excess maple mixture. Discard any remaining marinade. Arrange beef in single layer on racks. Cook on separate racks in 170°F (77°C) oven for about 8 hours, turning strips and switching position of baking sheets at halftime, until dried. Store in air-tight container for up to 2 weeks. Makes about 1 lb. (454 g).

2 oz. (57 g): 187 Calories; 3.6 g Total Fat (1.5 g Mono, 0.2 g Poly, 1.2 g Sat); 46 mg Cholesterol; 11 g Carbohydrate; trace Fibre; 26 g Protein; 678 mg Sodium

Pictured at right.

Note: To slice meat easily, place in freezer for about 30 minutes until just starting to freeze. If using from frozen state, partially thaw before cutting.

Honey Ginger Barbecue Sauce

Dad loves to grill, and you love to eat—so this homemade barbecue sauce makes the perfect gift for both of you! Goes great with any choice of grilled meat or vegetables.

Sesame (or cooking) oil	1 tbsp	15 mL
Finely chopped onion	1/2 cup	125 mL
Garlic cloves, minced (or 3/4 tsp., 4 mL, powder)	3	3
Cans of tomato sauce (14 oz., 398 mL, each)	2	2
Apple cider vinegar	1/2 cup	125 mL
Liquid honey	1/2 cup	125 mL
Soy sauce	1/3 cup	75 mL
Finely grated ginger root	2 tbsp.	30 mL
Hoisin sauce	2 tbsp.	30 mL
Sweet smoked paprika	1 tbsp.	15 mL
Pepper	1 tsp.	5 mL

Heat sesame oil in medium saucepan on medium. Add onion and garlic. Cook for about 5 minutes, stirring often, until onion is softened.

Add remaining 8 ingredients. Stir. Bring to a boil. Reduce heat to medium-low. Simmer, uncovered, for 20 minutes, stirring occasionally, to blend flavours. Fill 5 hot sterile 1 cup (250 mL) jars with tight-fitting lids. Make up to 1 month ahead; store for up to 3 weeks, and refrigerate after opening. Makes about 4 7/8 cups (1.2 L).

1 tbsp. (15 mL): 14 Calories; 0.2 g Total Fat (0 g Mono, 0 g Poly, trace Sat); 0 mg Cholesterol; 3 g Carbohydrate; trace Fibre; trace Protein; 157 mg Sodium

Pictured at right.

Clockwise from Left:
Honey Ginger Barbecue Sauce, above
Round-The-World Barbecue Blast, this page
Superhero Beef Jerky, this page

King of the Grill Apron

If the barbecue is Dad's domain, give him a gift that he'll really put to good use. This apron has a handy pocket and a loop for holding Dad's favourite barbecue tools. A sewing machine is required to put this project together.

MATERIALS
7 x 15 inch (18 x 38 cm) piece of denim fabric
4 1/2 x 2 inch (11 x 5 cm) piece of denim fabric
7 x 15 inch (18 x 38 cm) piece of flame-coloured fabric
7 x 7 inch (18 x 18 cm) piece of yellow or gold fabric
Adult-sized white apron
17 x 12 inch (43 cm x 30 cm) piece of iron-on adhesive
  (no-sew)
5 star-shaped buttons or jewels
Iron-on letters to spell "KING" (optional)
3-D shiny black fabric paint

TOOLS
pins, iron, needle, white and blue thread, scissors, ruler,
  pencil, sewing machine, cardboard

Wash and dry fabric and apron, without fabric softener. Enlarge the crown and flame patterns by 200%.

Take the 7 x 15 inch (18 x 38 cm) piece of denim fabric, and make a 1/2 inch (12 mm) hem on all 4 sides by folding in 1/4 inch (6 mm) raw edge. Iron. Fold in another 1/4 inch (6 mm) edge on all 4 sides and iron. Sew the edge of one of the 15 inch (38 cm) sides with 1/8 inch (3 mm) seam allowance. This will be the top of the pocket. Find the middle of your apron and pin the pocket at the desired height. Sew the bottom and sides of the pocket onto the apron. Remove pins.

(continued on next page)

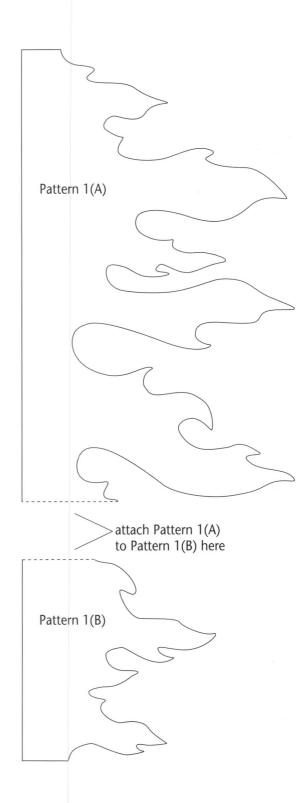

Pattern 1(A)

attach Pattern 1(A)
to Pattern 1(B) here

Pattern 1(B)

Take the 4 1/2 x 2 inch (11 x 5 cm) piece of denim fabric, fold in a 1/4 inch (6 mm) edge on all 4 sides and iron. Sew close to the edge on both 4 1/2 inch (11 cm) sides. This will be the tool band. Pin the band at the desired height and side of apron. Use your barbecue tools to help with placement. Attach the band to the apron by sewing the 2 short ends to the apron.

Tape pattern pieces 1(A) and 1(B) together at dotted line to form 1 piece. Lay out iron-on adhesive on work surface, paper-side down. Place the flame-coloured fabric over the adhesive, right-side up, and place the flame pattern over top. Pin all 3 layers together and cut. Before removing pins, turn over so that the pattern is on the bottom and the paper of the iron-on adhesive is on top. Following the manufacturer's instructions, iron in several places, just to keep iron-on adhesive in place once you remove the pattern pins. Let cool. Remove pins and pattern and continue to iron. Fold down the pocket and pin the flames to the apron, just inside the pocket. Attach the flames to apron using the iron, following the manufacturer's instructions.

Follow the above steps with the crown pattern (Pattern 2), the yellow or gold fabric and more iron-on adhesive. Place the crown at the top centre of the apron. Iron the crown to the apron following the manufacturer's instructions. Sew the buttons to the points of the crown.

Attach the iron-on letters to the crown, following manufacturer's instructions. Place the cardboard underneath the apron. With fabric paint, decorate the crown. Underneath the iron-on letters, write "of the Grill" on the apron with fabric paint (see photo).

Pictured at left.

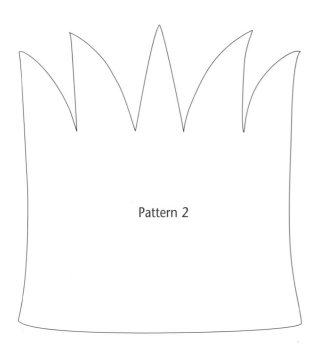

Pattern 2

Sweet Chili Sauce

Sweet chili sauce is all the rage. Give Dad this special homemade version so he can spice up all his favourite foods. It pairs well with all the usual suspects, but it's particularly good with grilled meats and vegetables.

Granulated sugar	2 cups	500 mL
Water	1 cup	250 mL
White vinegar	1 cup	250 mL
Garlic cloves, minced	4	4
Thai hot chili peppers, halved (see Tip, page 67)	6	6
Water	2 tbsp.	30 mL

Combine first 3 ingredients in small saucepan. Bring to a boil, stirring occasionally, until sugar is dissolved. Reduce heat to medium. Boil gently for about 25 minutes until syrup consistency.

Process remaining 3 ingredients in blender or food processor until well combined. Add to sugar mixture. Stir. Pour into 4 sterile 1/2 cup (125 mL) jars with tight-fitting lids. Make up to 1 month ahead; store for up to 3 weeks, and refrigerate after opening. Makes about 2 cups (500 mL).

1 tbsp. (15 mL): 50 Calories; trace Total Fat (0 g Mono, trace Poly, 0 g Sat); 0 mg Cholesterol; 13 g Carbohydrate; trace Fibre; trace Protein; 1 mg Sodium

Pictured below.

Peppermint Trinity Cookies

These delicious Christmas cookies boast bright holiday colours for a truly festive look. You must use paste food colouring to get the really bright colours. Use these cookies for the Advent Calendar, at right, for a small holiday treat each day.

All-purpose flour	1 1/2 cups	375 mL
Cornstarch	1/2 cup	125 mL
Butter (or hard margarine), softened	1 cup	250 mL
Icing (confectioner's) sugar	2/3 cup	150 mL
Peppermint extract	1 tsp.	5 mL
Green paste food colouring (see Note)	1/4 tsp.	1 mL
Red paste food colouring (see Note)	1/4 tsp.	1 mL
White sanding (decorating) sugar (see Tip, page 112)	2 tbsp.	30 mL
Green sanding (decorating) sugar (see Tip, page 112)	1 tbsp.	15 mL
Red sanding (decorating) sugar (see Tip, page 112)	1 tbsp.	15 mL
Egg white (large), fork-beaten	1	1

Combine flour and cornstarch in small bowl. Set aside.

Beat next 3 ingredients in medium bowl until light and fluffy. Add flour mixture in 2 additions, mixing well after each addition until no dry flour remains. Divide dough into 3 equal portions.

Knead green food colouring into 1 dough portion. Knead red food colouring into 1 dough portion. Roll each portion into 10 inch (25 cm) rope. Lay 2 ropes side by side. Place remaining rope on top. Press together and roll into 12 inch (30 cm) log.

Combine next 3 ingredients in small bowl. Spread evenly on sheet of waxed paper, slightly longer than log. Brush log evenly with egg white. Roll in sanding sugar until coated. Wrap with plastic wrap. Chill for at least 4 hours. Discard plastic wrap. Cut log into 1/4 inch (6 mm) slices. Arrange slices, about 1 inch (2.5 cm) apart, on greased cookie sheets. Bake in 350°F (175°C) oven for about 10 minutes until golden. Let stand on cookie sheets for 5 minutes before removing to wire rack to cool. Cool cookie sheets between batches. Makes about 36 cookies.

1 cookie: 84 Calories; 5.1 g Total Fat (1.3 g Mono, 0.2 g Poly, 3.2 g Sat); 13 mg Cholesterol; 9 g Carbohydrate; trace Fibre; 1 g Protein; 38 mg Sodium

Pictured on page 32.

Note: These cookies can be made with liquid food colouring— just be sure to use only a few drops or the dough will be too wet. The colour will be paler.

Advent Calendar

Store-bought advent calendars lack the personal touch that is so important during the holidays. Fill the pockets on this advent calendar with individually wrapped cookies and let the countdown begin. This project doesn't require sewing, so it can be a fun one to do with the kids!

MATERIALS
12 x 18 inch (30 x 45 cm) piece of stiff green felt
2 sheets of red felt
2 sheets of white felt
Sheet of gold felt
Velvet number stickers
Green chenille stem (6 inch, 15 cm, length)

TOOLS
ruler, pen, scissors, felt glue, pins, hole punch

Enlarge all patterns by 200%. Cut out along solid lines. With a ruler, find the middle of the short side of the green felt. Line up the dotted line of Pattern 1 with the middle of the felt sheet. Trace the pattern along the solid lines using a pen. Do not trace along dotted line. Turn the pattern over and repeat on the other half of the felt sheet. Cut the felt pattern out. Using the star pattern, trace and cut 2 stars (Pattern 2) from the gold felt.

Trace and cut 7 white and 8 red felt circles (Pattern 3). With Pattern 4, trace and cut 7 red and 8 white felt ornament toppers. Glue the toppers to the circles, putting the red toppers on the white circles and the white toppers on the red circles. Let dry. Position 8 ornaments on 1 side of the tree, leaving 7 for the other side. Apply a fine bead of glue around the back outside edge of the bottom 2/3 of each ornament, leaving the top 1/3 open to form pockets. Attach ornaments to tree. Let dry. Repeat with remaining ornaments on other side of tree.

For ornament hangers, cut very thin white strips of felt, about 3 inches (7.5 cm) long. Pin back the top of each ornament and glue 1 strip, formed into a loop, to each ornament. Let dry. Remove pins.

With the scissors, cut ten 2 x 3 inch (5 x 7.5 cm) rectangles from red felt. Use scrap pieces of felt to decorate the rectangles like presents, keeping in mind that you will be attaching numbers to them. Position 5 presents on 1 side of the base of the tree. Apply a fine bead of glue to the back of each present along 3 edges, leaving the top 3 inch (7.5 cm) side open. Attach presents to tree. Let dry. Repeat with remaining presents on other side of tree.

Arrange numbers 1 to 25 over the ornaments and presents. Stick onto calendar.

(continued on next page)

Make a hole in the top centre of the tree using the hole punch. Loop the chenille stem through the hole and twist ends to secure. Glue the 2 stars together with 1 on each side of the tree, making sure the chenille loop is between and exposed above the stars. Let dry.

Pictured on page 32.

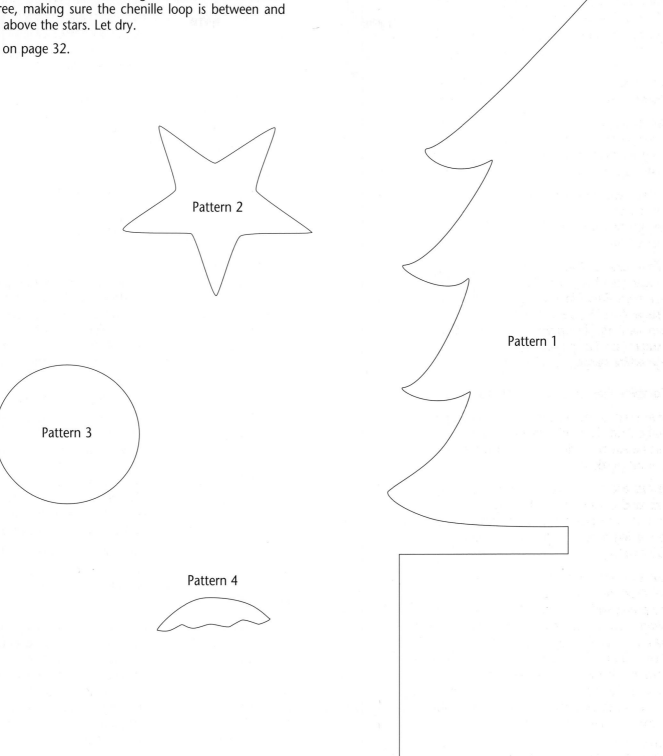

Pattern 2

Pattern 1

Pattern 3

Pattern 4

Almond Snowballs

If you're dreaming of a white Christmas, these pristine snowballs made from white chocolate are just the thing. With hints of coconut and almond, they're packed with flavour and make an attractive addition to a tray of goodies. They're even sturdy enough to ship for long-distance gift exchanges.

White chocolate bar, chopped	3 1/2 oz.	100 g
Almond liqueur	1 tbsp.	15 mL
Coconut extract	1/2 tsp.	2 mL
Crisp rice cereal	1/4 cup	60 mL
Whole natural almonds, cut in half and toasted (see Tip, page 34)	6	6
White candy melting wafers	1/2 cup	125 mL
Fine coconut	1/3 cup	75 mL

Put chocolate into small microwave-safe bowl. Microwave on medium (50%), stirring every 15 seconds, until almost melted. Add liqueur and extract. Stir until smooth. Add cereal. Stir well. Roll into balls, using about 2 tsp. (10 mL) for each.

Push 1 almond half into centre of each ball. Roll balls to enclose almonds in chocolate mixture. Arrange on waxed paper-lined baking sheet.

Put candy wafers into small microwave-safe cup (see Tip, page 12). Microwave, uncovered, on medium (50%), stirring every 15 seconds, until almost melted. Stir until smooth.

Put coconut into small shallow dish. Place 1 ball on end of wooden pick. Dip into chocolate until completely coated, allowing excess to drip back into cup. Roll in coconut until coated. Place on same waxed paper-lined baking sheet. Remove wooden pick. Repeat with remaining balls and chocolate (see Tip, page 154). Let stand for about 5 minutes until chocolate is set. Makes about 12 snowballs.

1 snowball: 107 Calories; 6.3 g Total Fat (0.8 g Mono, 0.2 g Poly, 4.1 g Sat); 4 mg Cholesterol; 10 g Carbohydrate; trace Fibre; 1 g Protein; 21 mg Sodium

Pictured at right.

Almond Snowballs, left

Topiary Truffles

Rather than ordinary glass balls and ornaments, these mini truffles make an attractive and delicious decoration for the Topiary Truffle Tree, at right.

Chocolate wafer crumbs	3/4 cups	175 mL
Whole natural almonds, toasted (see Tip, below)	2 tbsp.	30 mL
Icing (confectioner's) sugar	3 tbsp.	50 mL
Almond liqueur	2 tbsp.	30 mL
Corn syrup	1 1/2 tsp.	7 mL
Green candy melting wafers	1/2 cup	125 mL
Red candy melting wafers	1/2 cup	125 mL

Process wafer crumbs and almonds in blender or food processor until mixture resembles fine crumbs. Add icing sugar. Process for 1 minute. Add liqueur and corn syrup. Process until smooth. Transfer to small bowl. Let stand, covered, for about 1 hour until firm. Roll into 1/2 inch (12 mm) balls, using 1/4 tsp. (1 mL) for each. Place on waxed, paper-lined baking sheet.

Put green candy wafers into small microwave-safe cup (see Tip, page 12). Microwave, uncovered, on medium (50%), stirring every 15 seconds, until almost melted. Stir until smooth. Place 1 ball on wooden pick. Dip ball into melted wafers, allowing excess to drip back into bowl. Place on same waxed paper-lined baking sheet. Remove wooden pick. Repeat with 31 more balls. Repeat with red candy wafers and remaining balls (see Tip, page 154). Place on same baking sheet. Let stand until set. Makes about 65 truffles.

1 truffle: 33 Calories; 1.7 g Total Fat (0.4 g Mono, 0.1 g Poly, 0.9 g Sat); 1 mg Cholesterol; 4 g Carbohydrate; trace Fibre; trace Protein; 11 mg Sodium

Pictured at right.

Tip: When toasting whole natural almonds, place small amounts in ungreased shallow frying pan. Heat on medium for 3 to 5 minutes, stirring often, until skins darken slightly. For larger amounts, spread almonds evenly in an ungreased pan. Bake in a 350°F (175°C) oven for 5 to 10 minutes, stirring or shaking often until skins darken slightly.

Topiary Truffle Tree

This little tree is decorated with yummy truffles for an impressive Christmas gift that you will be truly proud to give.

MATERIALS
Dry florist foam (3 x 2 inch, 7.5 x 5 inch, piece)
Painted terra cotta pot (3 inch, 7.5 cm, diameter)
2 dowels (1/4 inch, 6 mm, diameter), 6 inches (15 cm) long
3 inch (7.5 cm) foam ball
6 x 10 inch (15 x 25 cm) sheet of foil
Topiary Truffles, at left
Wooden picks
Piece of ribbon (6 inches, 15 cm, long)
Snowflake stickers (optional)
Spanish moss

TOOLS
sharp knife, glue gun

With knife, cut and shape florist foam to fit snugly inside the pot, making sure it fits below the rim by about 1/4 inch (6 mm). Secure the foam with glue. Insert dowels into centre of florist foam. Wrap foam ball with foil, trimming bottom if necessary. Centre ball over dowels and push the ball halfway onto the dowels.

Place truffles on ends of wooden picks and arrange randomly over ball. Tie ribbon around the dowels at the bottom of the ball.

Decorate the pot with snowflake stickers. Use a little glue on the florist foam to secure the Spanish moss over it.

Pictured at right.

Vanilla Brandy Liqueur

Holiday spirits make a special Christmas gift—especially when you've made them yourself! This lovely vanilla liqueur is delicious served over ice or as an addition to coffee or tea. A thoughtful gift that's sure to add a little holiday cheer to any get-together.

Vanilla beans	4	4
Brandy (see Tip, page 87)	3 cups	750 mL
Granulated sugar	1 cup	250 mL
Water	1/2 cup	125 mL

Split vanilla beans lengthwise. Do not remove seeds. Put into 1 quart (1 L) jar with tight-fitting lid. Add brandy. Let stand at room temperature for 4 weeks. Strain through 4 layers of cheesecloth into 4 cup (1 L) liquid measure. Discard solids. Return brandy mixture to same jar.

Bring sugar and water to a boil in small saucepan, stirring until sugar is dissolved. Remove from heat. Cool to room temperature. Add to brandy mixture. Seal jar. Let stand at room temperature for 4 weeks. Pour into sterile jars or decorative bottles with tight-fitting lids. Makes about 4 cups (1 L).

1 oz. (30 mL): 85 Calories; 0 g Total Fat (0 g Mono, 0 g Poly, 0 g Sat); 0 mg Cholesterol; 6 g Carbohydrate; 0 g Fibre; 0 g Protein; trace Sodium

Pictured at right and on page 159.

Whiskey River Fudge

Fudge with an Irish attitude—perfect for all the grown-ups with its delicious whiskey flavour. This is one fudge recipe that's not for the kids!

Miniature marshmallows	4 cups	1 L
Granulated sugar	1 1/2 cups	375 mL
Evaporated milk	2/3 cup	150 mL
Butter	1/4 cup	60 mL
Salt	1/4 tsp.	1 mL
Milk chocolate chips	1 1/2 cups	375 mL
White chocolate chips	1 cup	250 mL
Irish whiskey	1/4 cup	60 mL

Line 9 x 9 inch (22 x 22 cm) pan with greased foil, leaving 1 inch (2.5 cm) overhang on 2 sides. Set aside. Combine first 5 ingredients in large saucepan. Heat and stir on medium until boiling and sugar is dissolved. Boil for 5 minutes, stirring constantly. Remove from heat.

Add remaining 3 ingredients. Stir until smooth. Spread evenly in prepared pan. Let stand in pan at least 8 hours or overnight until firm. Holding foil, remove fudge from pan. Cut into 64 squares.

1 square: 80 Calories; 3.2 g Total Fat (0.7 g Mono, 0.1 g Poly, 1.9 g Sat); 5 mg Cholesterol; 12 g Carbohydrate; trace Fibre; 1 g Protein; 26 mg Sodium

Pictured at right.

Variation: Try using rye, scotch or bourbon whiskey instead of Irish whiskey.

On Plate:
Left: Whiskey River Fudge, above
Right: Vanilla Brandy Liqueur, this page

Random Acts of Kindness Week

Each year, the second week of February is set aside for a very special occasion that many people aren't even aware of—Random Acts of Kindness Week. The concept behind this occasion is simple: perform selfless acts of kindness for others. You may choose to do something completely spontaneous for a complete stranger. Or you may plan this kind act long in advance for someone you've known all your life. The result? The individual you have helped is happier, and you feel good for having done something thoughtful for another person.

A random act of kindness doesn't need to be an extravagant gift, and it doesn't require a huge investment of your time. Sometimes simply smiling or saying hello to a stranger is all you need. However, if you want to add a more personal touch, you could bring a container of freshly baked cookies into the office, or make a special treat for an unsuspecting friend. All these things add a little more joy to the world.

Kitchen gifts are a great way to spread the joy during Random Acts of Kindness Week. You could prepare seven different recipes, or make one big batch and divide it into portions that can be given to someone different each day of the week. Dry mixes and sweets work particularly well for week-long giving.

Remember that you aren't limited to performing random acts of kindness during this one week of the year. You can perform a simple act of kindness each day, and the world will be a much happier place for it!

White Chocolate Cookies

Show someone special that you're thinking about them with these delicate, dainty sandwich cookies. A perfect little treat to give a friend or co-worker for Random Acts of Kindness Week, or any other time you'd like to add a bit of sparkle to someone's day.

Butter (or hard margarine), softened	2/3 cup	150 mL
Icing (confectioner's) sugar	1/4 cup	60 mL
All-purpose flour	2 cups	500 mL
Milk	3 tbsp.	50 mL
Granulated sugar	1/4 cup	60 mL
WHITE CHOCOLATE FILLING		
White chocolate chips	1/4 cup	60 mL
Milk	1 tbsp.	15 mL
Butter (or hard margarine), softened	1 tbsp.	15 mL
Icing (confectioner's) sugar	1 1/4 cups	300 mL

Beat butter and sugar in large bowl until light and fluffy. Add flour and milk. Mix well. Roll out dough on lightly floured surface to 1/8 inch (3 mm) thickness. Cut out shapes with lightly floured 1 1/2 inch (3.8 cm) circle-shaped cookie cutter. Roll out scraps to cut more shapes. Arrange half of circles, 1 inch (2.5 cm) apart, on ungreased cookie sheets.

Sprinkle sugar evenly on sheet of waxed paper. Gently press both sides of remaining circles into sugar until coated. Arrange, 1 inch (2.5 cm) apart, on ungreased cookie sheets. Prick sugared circles 4 times with fork to form square shape in centre of cookies. Bake in 375°F (190°C) oven for about 7 minutes until golden on bottom. Let stand on cookie sheets for 5 minutes before removing to wire racks to cool. Cool cookie sheets between batches

White Chocolate Filling: Combine chocolate chips and milk in small microwave-safe bowl. Microwave, on medium (50%), stirring every 15 seconds, until almost melted. Stir until smooth.

Beat butter and icing sugar in medium bowl until smooth. Add chocolate mixture. Beat well. Makes about 1/2 cup (125 mL) filling. Spoon into piping bag fitted with small plain tip or small resealable freezer bag with tiny piece snipped off corner. Pipe about 1/2 tsp (2 mL) filling onto bottom of each plain cookie. Place sugared cookies over filling. Makes about 38 sandwich cookies.

1 sandwich cookie: 84 Calories; 4.0 g Total Fat (0.9 g Mono, 0.1 g Poly, 2.5 g Sat); 10 mg Cholesterol; 12 g Carbohydrate; trace Fibre; 1 g Protein; 27 mg Sodium

Pictured at right.

Left: Chocolate Almond Brittle, right
Right: White Chocolate Cookies, above

Chocolate Almond Brittle

This simple sweet takes only a short time to put together, but it's sure to bring a whole lot of happiness when you give it as an unexpected gift. Perfect for any occasion or as a random gift for someone special.

Chopped slivered almonds, toasted (see Tip, page 41)	1/2 cup	125 mL
Mini semi-sweet chocolate chips	1/2 cup	125 mL
Butter	1 cup	250 mL
Granulated sugar	1 cup	250 mL
Water	2 tbsp.	30 mL
Golden corn syrup	1 tbsp.	15 mL

Sprinkle almonds and chocolate chips evenly in greased 9 x 13 inch (22 x 33 cm) baking pan.

Combine remaining 4 ingredients in medium heavy saucepan. Heat and stir on medium until mixture comes to a boil. Boil for about 10 minutes, stirring often, until mixture reaches soft crack stage (about 270°F, 132°C) on candy thermometer (see Tip, page 77) or until small amount dropped into very cold water separates into hard, but pliable, threads. Carefully pour mixture over almonds and chocolate chips. Spread evenly. Chill for about 1 hour until set. Break into pieces. Makes about 24 pieces.

1 piece: 132 Calories; 9.8 g Total Fat (3.0 g Mono, 0.6 g Poly, 5.5 g Sat); 20 mg Cholesterol; 12 g Carbohydrate; trace Fibre; 1 g Protein; 56 mg Sodium

Pictured below.

Special Occasions

Maybe it's an event that happens often, or just once in a lifetime—whatever the case, these special occasions deserve to be marked. Give a special friend a creative birthday gift, or celebrate the arrival of a new baby with a delicious kitchen gift. You'll find ideas for personalized anniversary gifts, convenient treats for moving day, must-have nibbles for the first day at a new job, and even a few goodies for the family pet.

Pirates' Delight Liqueur

Yar matey! This spiced rum concoction would please any pirate on the high seas—and it's sure to please any of your friends lucky enough to receive this as a special birthday gift!

Vanilla bean	1/2	1/2
Amber (golden) rum (see Tip, page 87)	3 cups	750 mL
Cinnamon sticks (4 inches, 10 cm, each)	4	4
Whole nutmeg (optional)	1	1
Star anise	2	2
Whole cloves	5	5
Brown sugar, packed	2/3 cup	150 mL
Water	1/3 cup	75 mL

Split vanilla bean lengthwise. Do not remove seeds. Put into sterile 4 cup (1 L) jar with tight-fitting lid.

Add next 5 ingredients. Seal. Let stand at room temperature for 2 weeks. Strain through sieve into 4 cup (1 L) liquid measure. Discard solids. Return rum mixture to same jar.

Combine sugar and water in small saucepan. Bring to a boil, stirring constantly until sugar is dissolved. Cool. Add to rum mixture. Seal jar. Let stand at room temperature for 2 weeks. Strain through 4 layers of cheesecloth into 4 cup (1 L) liquid measure. Discard solids. Pour into sterile jars or decorative bottles with tight-fitting lids. Makes about 3 2/3 cups (900 mL).

1 oz. (30 mL): 80 Calories; 0.0 g Total Fat (0.0 g Mono, 0.0 g Poly, 0.0 g Sat); 0 mg Cholesterol; 5 g Carbohydrate; 0 g Fibre; 0 g Protein; 2 mg Sodium

Pictured at right.

> **Tip:** When toasting nuts, seeds or coconut, cooking times will vary for each type of nut—so never toast them together. For small amounts, place ingredient in an ungreased shallow frying pan. Heat on medium for 3 to 5 minutes, stirring often, until golden. For larger amounts, spread ingredient evenly in an ungreased pan. Bake in a 350°F (175°C) oven for 5 to 10 minutes, stirring or shaking often, until golden.

Almond Pretzel Bark

This sweet and salty pretzel bark makes a perfect birthday gift for a friend or coworker who's got a serious chocolate addiction.

Dark chocolate melting wafers	3 cups	750 mL
Stick pretzels, broken in half	2 cups	500 mL
Slivered almonds, toasted (see Tip, this page)	1 1/2 cups	375 mL
White candy melting wafers	2 tbsp.	30 mL

Heat chocolate wafers in heavy medium saucepan on lowest heat for about 6 minutes, stirring often, until almost melted. Remove from heat. Stir until smooth. Add pretzels and almonds. Stir well. Spread evenly in 10 x 15 inch (25 x 38 cm) parchment (not waxed) paper-lined baking sheet with sides.

Put candy wafers into small microwave-safe cup. Microwave, uncovered, on medium (50%), stirring every 15 seconds, until almost melted. Stir until smooth. Drizzle over pretzel mixture. Chill for about 1 hour until firm. Break into irregular-shaped pieces. Makes about 24 pieces.

1 piece: 170 Calories; 10.5 g Total Fat (4.5 g Mono, 1.1 g Poly, 4.4 g Sat); trace Cholesterol; 20 g Carbohydrate; 2 g Fibre; 3 g Protein; 76 mg Sodium

Pictured below.

Left: Almond Pretzel Bark, above; Right: Pirates' Delight Liqueur, this page

Cocoa Pecan Crispbread

Crisp crackers full of pecans and a hint of Mexican molé spices. For an extra-special birthday gift, package it with a bag of specialty coffee and a couple of mugs, or with Mixed-Up Mojito Mix, at right.

All-purpose flour	3/4 cup	175 mL
Cocoa, sifted if lumpy	1 tbsp.	15 mL
Chili powder	1/2 tsp.	2 mL
Ground cinnamon	1/2 tsp.	2 mL
Cayenne pepper	1/8 tsp.	0.5 mL
Egg whites (large), room temperature	3	3
Brown sugar, packed	1/3 cup	75 mL
Cream of tartar	1/8 tsp.	0.5 mL
Pecan halves	1 1/2 cups	375 mL

Combine first 5 ingredients in small bowl.

Beat next 3 ingredients in medium bowl for about 6 minutes until stiff peaks form. Fold in flour mixture until no dry flour remains.

Fold in pecans. Spread evenly in greased 9 x 5 x 3 inch (22 x 12.5 x 7.5 cm) loaf pan lined with parchment (not waxed) paper. Bake in 350°F (175°C) oven for about 25 minutes until firm. Let stand in pan on wire rack for 45 minutes. Using serrated knife, cut into 1/8 inch (3 mm) slices. Arrange on greased baking sheets. Bake in 300°F (150°C) oven for about 20 minutes, turning at halftime, until dry and crisp. Let stand on baking sheets on wire racks until cool. Makes about 52 crisps.

1 crisp: 34 Calories; 2.3 g Total Fat (1.3 g Mono, 0.7 g Poly, 0.2 g Sat); 0 mg Cholesterol; 3 g Carbohydrate; trace Fibre; 1 g Protein; 4 mg Sodium

Pictured on page 45.

Mixed-Up Mojito Mix

The refreshing flavours of this citrusy non-alcoholic cocktail can be enjoyed any time. Just add to a bottle of water and shake.

Rum extract	1 1/2 tsp.	7 mL
Granulated sugar	1/2 cup	125 mL
Granulated sugar	1/2 cup	125 mL
Peppermint extract	3/4 tsp.	4 mL
Unsweetened lemon-lime powdered drink mix	1/4 oz.	6 g

Drizzle rum extract over first amount of sugar in bowl. Stir well. Spread sugar evenly on sheet of waxed paper.

Repeat on separate sheet of waxed paper with remaining sugar and peppermint extract. Let stand for about 3 hours until dry.

Combine drink mix and rum and peppermint sugar in small bowl. Spoon into 5 small resealable freezer bags. Makes about 1 1/4 cups (300 mL).

Pictured on pages 43 and 45.

Directions for Mixed-Up Mojito:

Empty contents of bag into 16 oz. (500 mL) bottle of water. Seal. Shake until dissolved. Makes 2 cups (500 mL).

2 cups (500 mL) mojito: 160 Calories; 0.0 g Total Fat (0.0 g Mono, 0.0 g Poly, 0.0 g Sat); 0 mg Cholesterol; 40 g Carbohydrate; 0 g Fibre; 0 g Protein; 14 mg Sodium

---

How To

Wallet Packages

This wallet is a really quick way to package up a small amount of dry ingredients. These instructions make two wallets to place inside the Purse Bag, page 44.

MATERIALS
12 x 12 inch (30 x 30 cm) sheet of cardstock
4 brads
Embroidery floss
Dry drink mix
Snack-sized resealable bags

TOOLS
scissors, pencil

Enlarge pattern by 200%. Trace pattern and all markings onto the wrong side of cardstock and cut. Fold in on dotted lines. Insert a brad at each 'X'. Tie the embroidery floss to the brad on the flap. Trim ends.

Put dry mix into snack-sized resealable bags, and include directions. Fold in half and place inside wallet. Fold over package and wrap floss in a figure-eight around the 2 brads. Repeat to make second wallet.

Pictured below and on page 45.

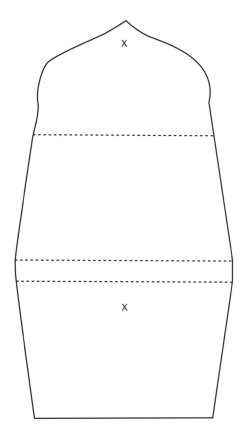

Centre: Wallet Packages, above
Left and Right: Mixed-Up Mojito Mix, left

How To

Purse Bag

This is a fun gift bag for that girlfriend who just loves to shop.

MATERIALS
Two 12 inch (30 cm) squares of cardstock
Lightweight cardboard (or cereal) box
8 1/2 x 11 inch (21 x 28 cm) piece of coordinating cardstock
2 silver eyelets
Velcro circle
Piece of narrow ribbon (12 inches, 30 cm, long)

TOOLS
pencil, scissors, ruler, scoring tool, fast-grab tacky glue,
  eyelet setting tools

Cut two 8 1/4 x 9 1/4 inch (21 x 23 cm) pieces from the 12 inch (30 cm) squares of cardstock. These will be the front and back of your bag. Take the 2 remaining 3 3/4 inch (9 cm) pieces and shorten them to 9 1/4 inch (23 cm) long. These will be the sides of your bag.

Take the front and back pieces and score on the dotted lines following Diagram A. Fold the paper in at the top and bottom. Fold in the sides down to the 3 inch (7.5 cm) line. Take the two bottom corners, one at a time, and fold up to the 3 inch (7.5 cm) line. Cut with scissors from the 3/4 inch (2 cm) line to the 3 inch (7.5 cm) line (see photo).

Following Diagram B, score the side pieces on the dotted lines. Fold in along the 1 inch (2.5 cm) and 3 inch (7.5 cm) lines. Then fold in the middle, in the opposite direction, so that other folds are to the outside.

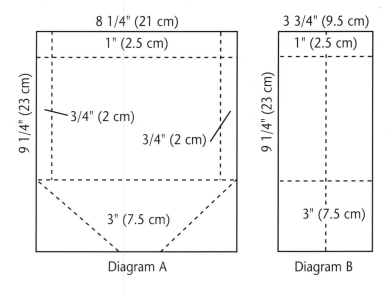

Diagram A

Diagram B

Glue the side pieces to the outside of the 3/4 inch (2 cm) tabs on the front and back pieces. Do one corner at a time, folding the top 1 inch (2.5 cm) flap of the side pieces over the 3/4 inch (2 cm) tabs of the front and back pieces. Fold the 3 inch (7.5 cm) bottom flap under the small triangle piece you cut out. Repeat with all corners. Glue down the 1 inch (2.5 cm) flaps on the sides of the bag. Glue the bottom flaps to the underside of the bag.

Enlarge the purse closure (Pattern 1) by 200%. Using the pattern piece, cut 1 piece from the lightweight cardboard and 2 from the coordinating cardstock. Glue the cardstock pieces to each side of the purse flap to cover the cardboard. Let dry. Following the diagram, score and fold on the dotted lines. Measure 2 inches (5 cm) between the fold lines on both sides and mark with pencil. Punch holes for handles. Set 2 eyelets, and string ribbon through eyelets; tie a knot at both ends. Glue the flap to the inside of the bag, just up to the first fold. Glue Velcro circles to the purse and the underside of purse flap.

Pictured on page 4 and at right.

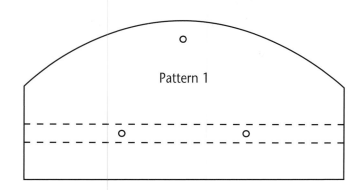

Pattern 1

Top: Purse Bag, above
Centre: Wallet Package, page 43,
with Mixed-Up Mojito Mix, page 42
Bottom: Cocoa Pecan Crispbread, page 42

Peppermint Hard Candies

These hard candies are unbelievably easy to make and will add an extra touch of sweetness to any couple's anniversary. Make these translucent mints in any colour by changing the shade of food colouring.

Granulated sugar	1 cup	250 mL
Water	1/2 cup	125 mL
White corn syrup	1/2 cup	125 mL
Mint and peppermint extract	1 tbsp.	15 mL
Drops of green liquid food colouring (optional)	4	4

Combine first 3 ingredients in small saucepan. Bring to a boil on medium, stirring occasionally. Boil for about 25 minutes without stirring, brushing sides of pan with wet pastry brush to dissolve any sugar crystals, until mixture reaches hard-crack stage (about 300°F, 150°C) on candy thermometer (see Tip, page 77) or until small amount dropped into very cold water separates into hard, brittle threads. Remove from heat.

Add extract and food colouring. Stir for 5 seconds. Transfer to microwave-safe glass measuring cup. Drop in 1 tsp. (5 mL) amounts onto 2 parchment (not waxed) paper-lined large baking sheets (see Note). Cool. Makes about 65 candies.

1 candy: 20 Calories; trace Total Fat (0.0 g Mono, 0.0 g Poly, 0.0 g Sat); 0 mg Cholesterol; 5 g Carbohydrate; 0 g Fibre; 0 g Protein; 2 mg Sodium

Pictured below.

Note: If mixture begins to thicken as it cools, microwave on high (100%) for about 20 seconds until pourable consistency.

Chocolate Passion Fondue Mix

Whether it's your anniversary or you're giving this gift to a special couple, this sinful fondue is just the way to celebrate the occasion. Goes great with fresh fruit, Candy Angel Dippers and Dipping Cookies, both on page 48. Give with a can of thick cream for a complete gift.

Dark chocolate bar, finely chopped	3 1/2 oz.	100 g
Milk chocolate bar, finely chopped	3 1/2 oz.	100 g
Orange liqueur	1 tbsp.	15 mL
White balsamic vinegar (see Note)	1 tbsp.	15 mL
Vanilla extract	1 tsp.	5 mL

Combine dark and milk chocolate in decorative cellophane bag.

Combine next 3 ingredients in small bowl. Pour into small decorative bottle.

Pictured on page 49.

Note: If white balsamic is unavailable, use 2 tsp. (10 mL) of regular balsamic vinegar instead.

Directions for Chocolate Passion Fondue:

Heat contents of bag and 6 oz. (170 mL) can of thick cream in medium heavy saucepan on lowest heat, stirring often, until chocolate is almost melted. Remove from heat. Add contents of bottle. Stir until smooth. Carefully pour into fondue pot. Keep warm over low flame. Serve with your choice of dippers. Makes about 1 1/2 cups (375 mL).

2 tbsp. (30 mL): 120 Calories; 7.6 g Total Fat (0.0 g Mono, 0.0 g Poly, 4.7 g Sat); 12 mg Cholesterol; 11 g Carbohydrate; 1 g Fibre; 1 g Protein; 10 mg Sodium

---

How To

Embossed Anniversary Box

Take a plain paper box and turn it into a beautiful package full of fondue dippers for a very special couple on their anniversary.

MATERIALS
Metallic black paint
Round paper mâché box with lid (7 inch, 18 cm, diameter)
Gold embossing powder
Watermark ink pad
Rubber stamps
12 inch (30 cm) square of red cardstock
12 inch (30 cm) square of cardstock with printed love messages (optional)
Gold ink pad

TOOLS
foam paint brush, craft tray, heat gun, fast-grab tacky glue

Paint box and lid with random brush stokes. Let dry. With your finger, brush a little gold powder onto the box and lid.

Apply ink to rubber stamp. Press stamps onto red cardstock, firmly and evenly. Generously sprinkle embossing powder over wet ink. Tap excess powder into craft tray and reuse. Melt embossing powder with heat gun. It will appear shiny and have texture when melted. Rip cardstock around the stamped images. Rip a few love messages from the other piece of cardstock (see photo).

With the gold ink pad, brush the edges of the cardstock pieces where you've ripped them. Glue the stamped pieces onto the sides of the box. Randomly glue love messages to the lid.

Pictured on page 49.

Dipping Cookies

Cookies make the perfect dipper for a dessert fondue. We've selected this delicious cookie as a companion for our Chocolate Passion Fondue, page 47, and wrapped it all up in an Embossed Anniversary Box, page 47, for one lucky couple to share.

Butter (or hard margarine), softened	2 tbsp.	30 mL
Granulated sugar	1/4 cup	60 mL
Milk	2 tbsp.	30 mL
Cooking oil	1 tsp.	5 mL
Vanilla extract	1/8 tsp.	0.5 mL
All-purpose flour	2/3 cup	150 mL
Baking powder	1/2 tsp.	2 mL
Salt	1/8 tsp.	0.5 mL
Baking soda, just a pinch		

Combine butter and sugar in medium bowl. Add next 3 ingredients. Stir well.

Combine remaining 4 ingredients in separate small bowl. Add to sugar mixture. Stir until no dry flour remains. Shape into disc. Wrap with plastic wrap. Chill for at least 1 hour. Discard plastic wrap. Roll out on lightly floured surface to 1/4 inch (6 mm) thickness. Cut out shapes using lightly floured 2 inch (5 cm) circle-shaped cookie cutter. Cut circles in half. Roll out scraps to cut more shapes. Arrange cookies, about 1 inch (2.5 cm) apart, on greased cookie sheet. Bake in 375°F (190°C) oven for about 6 minutes until edges start to turn golden. Let stand on cookie sheet for 5 minutes before removing to wire racks to cool. Cool cookie sheets between batches. Makes about 46 cookies.

1 cookie: 15 Calories; 0.6 g Total Fat (0.2 g Mono, 0.1 g Poly, 0.3 g Sat); 1 mg Cholesterol; 2 g Carbohydrate; trace Fibre; 0.2 g Protein; 38 mg Sodium

Pictured at right.

Candy Angel Dippers

These delightful bites of cake have a firm texture for easy fondue dipping. Serve with Chocolate Passion Fondue, page 46, and dip to your heart's content.

All-purpose flour	1 cup	250 mL
Icing (confectioner's) sugar	1 cup	250 mL
Toffee bits (such as Skor)	1/4 cup	60 mL
Baking powder	2 tsp.	10 mL
Salt	1/8 tsp.	0.5 mL
Milk	1 cup	250 mL
Egg whites (large), room temperature	2	2

Combine first 5 ingredients in large bowl.

Put milk into small saucepan. Heat on medium, stirring constantly, until very hot and bubbles form around edge of saucepan. Add to flour mixture. Stir until smooth.

Beat egg whites in small bowl until stiff peaks form. Fold into flour mixture until no white streaks remain. Spread evenly in waxed paper-lined 9 x 13 inch (22 x 33 cm) pan. Bake in 350°F (175°C) oven for about 15 minutes until wooden pick inserted in centre of cake comes out clean. Let stand in pan until cool. Run knife around inside edges of pan to loosen cake. Invert onto cutting board. Discard wax paper. Cut into 1 inch (2.5 cm) squares. Makes about 96 dippers.

1 dipper: 14 Calories; 0.2 g Total Fat (trace Mono, 0.0 g Poly, 0.1 g Sat); 1 mg Cholesterol; 3 g Carbohydrate; trace Fibre; trace Protein; 20 mg Sodium

Pictured at right.

1. Embossed Anniversary Box, page 47
2. Candy Angel Dippers, above
3. Chocolate Passion Fondue, page 47
4. Dipping Cookies, this page

Raisin Tea Scones

If you're looking for a simple anniversary gift that doesn't cross too far into the romantic realm, gift these light-tasting raisin scones with a jar of Ginger Pear Jam, at right.

All-purpose flour	2 cups	500 mL
Granulated sugar	1/3 cup	75 mL
Baking powder	2 tsp.	10 mL
Salt	1/4 tsp.	1 mL
Cold butter (or hard margarine), cut up	1/3 cup	75 mL
Raisins (or currants)	1/2 cup	125 mL
Large egg	1	1
Buttermilk (or soured milk, see Tip, page 128)	3/4 cup	175 mL
Large egg, fork-beaten	1	1
Granulated sugar	1 tsp.	5 mL

Combine first 4 ingredients in large bowl. Cut in butter until mixture resembles coarse crumbs. Add raisins. Stir. Make a well in centre.

Whisk egg and buttermilk in small bowl. Add to well. Stir until soft dough forms. Turn out onto lightly floured surface. Knead 6 times. Transfer to greased baking sheet. Shape into 7 inch (18 cm) diameter circle. Score into 8 wedges.

Brush with egg. Sprinkle with second amount of sugar. Bake in 425°F (220°C) oven for 18 to 20 minutes until golden brown and wooden pick inserted in centre comes out clean. Let stand on baking sheet for 5 minutes before removing to wire rack to cool. Cuts into 8 wedges.

1 wedge: 251 Calories; 9.0 g Total Fat (2.5 g Mono, 0.5 g Poly, 5.3 g Sat); 75 mg Cholesterol; 38 g Carbohydrate; 1 g Fibre; 6 g Protein; 296 mg Sodium

Pictured at right.

Ginger Pear Jam

Treat a special couple to a tasty anniversary gift. With flavours of ginger and sweet, mellow pear, this zesty jam provides the perfect flavour complement for desserts, pancakes, muffins, and even roast pork.

Finely chopped peeled pear	3 cups	750 mL
Finely chopped ginger root	1/2 cup	125 mL
Apple juice	1/3 cup	75 mL
Lemon juice	3 tbsp.	50 mL
Box of pectin crystals	2 oz.	57 g
Granulated sugar	3 cups	750 mL
Minced crystallized ginger	1/4 cup	60 mL

Combine first 4 ingredients in large saucepan on medium. Bring to a boil. Boil gently, covered, for about 10 minutes, until ginger is softened.

Add pectin, stirring constantly.

Add sugar. Heat and stir until mixture comes to a hard boil. Boil for 1 minute, stirring constantly.

Add crystallized ginger. Stir. Remove from heat. Skim and discard foam. Stir for 5 minutes to suspend fruit. Fill 7 hot sterile 1/2 cup (125 mL) jars to within 1/4 inch (6 mm) of top. Wipe rims. Place sterile metal lids on jars and screw on metal bands fingertip tight. Do not over-tighten. Process in boiling water bath for 10 minutes (see Note). Remove jars. Let stand at room temperature until cool. Chill after opening. Makes about 3 3/4 cups (925 mL).

1 tbsp (15 mL): 46 Calories; trace Total Fat (0.0 g Mono, 0.0 g Poly, 0.0 g Sat); 0 mg Cholesterol; 12 g Carbohydrate; trace Fibre; trace Protein; trace Sodium

Pictured on page 40 and at right.

Note: Processing time is for elevations 1001 to 3000 feet (306 to 915 m) above sea level. Make adjustment for elevation in your area if necessary.

Left: Ginger Pear Jam, above
Right: Raisin Tea Scones, this page

Spiced Iced Mocha Mix

Giving a blender as a wedding gift? Include a jar of this drink mix along with Cocoa Cinnamon Rimmer, below. You could even include a bottle of Vanilla Brandy Liqueur, page 36, for a truly decadent after-dinner sipper.

Powdered coffee whitener	1 cup	250 mL
Brown sugar, packed	1/3 cup	75 mL
Cocoa, sifted if lumpy	2 tbsp.	30 mL
Instant coffee granules	2 tbsp.	30 mL
Ground cinnamon	1/8 tsp.	0.5 mL
Salt	1/8 tsp.	0.5 mL
Ground cloves, just a pinch		

Combine all 7 ingredients in small bowl. Spoon into jar with tight-fitting lid. Makes about 1 cup (250 mL).

Pictured at right.

Directions for Spiced Iced Mocha:

Put 1 cup (250 mL) milk (or water) into blender or food processor. Add contents of jar and 12 to 15 ice cubes. Process until thick and smooth. Makes about 3 cups (750 mL).

3/4 cup (175 mL) mocha: 239 Calories; 9.2 g Total Fat (0.5 g Mono, trace Poly, 8.0 g Sat); 4 mg Cholesterol; 36 g Carbohydrate; 1 g Fibre; 4 g Protein; 155 mg Sodium

Cocoa Cinnamon Rimmer

Make any cup of hot chocolate, coffee or mocha a special treat when you coat the rim of the mug with some of this simple sugar mixture.

Granulated sugar	1/4 cup	60 mL
Cocoa, sifted if lumpy	1 tsp.	5 mL
Ground cinnamon	1/4 tsp.	1 mL

Process all 3 ingredients in blender until combined. Spoon into jar with tight-fitting lid. Makes about 1/4 cup (60 mL).

Pictured at right.

Directions for Cocoa Cinnamon Rimmer:

Put 1 tbsp. (15 mL) water (or liqueur) onto small plate. Sprinkle about 1 tbsp. (15 mL) cocoa mixture onto separate small plate. Dip rim of mug into water. Press into cocoa mixture. Fill mug with hot or iced coffee.

1/2 tsp. (2 mL) rimmer: 7 Calories; trace Total Fat (0.0 g Mono, 0.0 g Poly, 0.0 g Sat); 0 mg Cholesterol; 2 g Carbohydrate; trace Fibre; trace Protein; 0 mg Sodium

Tropical Smoothie Mix

Give the newlyweds a Jamaican vacation—or at least some of the sweet flavours of Jamaica in a refreshing smoothie. Include this smoothie mix and a bottle of coconut rum with the gift of a new blender.

Frozen mango pieces, thawed	2 cups	500 mL
Can of frozen concentrated tropical fruit juice	12 1/2 oz.	355 mL
Granulated sugar	1/4 cup	60 mL

Process all 3 ingredients in blender until smooth. Makes about 2 1/2 cups (625 mL). Pour into sterile bottle with tight-fitting lid.

Pictured at right.

Directions for Tropical Smoothie Mix:

Empty contents of bottle into 9 x 9 inch (22 x 22 cm) baking pan lined with plastic wrap. Freeze overnight until set. Invert onto work surface. Discard plastic wrap. Cut into 1 inch (2.5 cm) squares. Store in resealable freezer bag.

Directions for Tropical Smoothie:

Process 4 drink mix cubes with 1/2 cup (125 mL) plain yogurt and 1/2 cup (125 mL) mango nectar in blender or food processor until thick and smooth. Serves 1.

1 serving: 198 Calories; trace Total Fat (trace Mono, trace Poly, trace Sat); 4 mg Cholesterol; 40 g Carbohydrate; trace Fibre; 8 g Protein; 139 mg Sodium

Directions for South Seas Smoothie:

Add 1 oz. (30 mL) coconut rum to Tropical Smoothie. Serves 1.

1 serving: 264 Calories; trace Total Fat (trace Mono, trace Poly, trace Sat); 4 mg Cholesterol; 40 g Carbohydrate; trace Fibre; 8 g Protein; 139 mg Sodium

Left: Spiced Iced Mocha Mix, this page
Bottom Centre: Cocoa Cinnamon Rimmer, this page
Right: Tropical Smoothie Mix, above

Sesame Snap Cookie Mix

If an electric mixer is your wedding gift of choice, why not include a cookie mix that the newlyweds can prepare and enjoy together?

Brown sugar, packed	1/2 cup	125 mL
All-purpose flour	1 1/4 cups	300 mL
Granulated sugar	1/2 cup	125 mL
Baking powder	1/2 tsp.	2 mL
Salt	1/4 tsp.	1 mL
Sesame seeds, toasted (see Tip, page 41)	1/3 cup	75 mL
Ground cinnamon	1/4 tsp.	1 mL
Ground nutmeg	1/4 tsp.	1 mL
Sesame seeds, toasted (see Tip, page 41)	1/3 cup	75 mL

Pack brown sugar evenly in bottom of jar with tight-fitting lid.

Combine next 4 ingredients in small bowl. Spoon over brown sugar. Pack down gently.

Combine next 3 ingredients in same small bowl. Spoon over flour mixture.

Put second amount of sesame seeds into small resealable freezer bag. Place on top of spice mixture. Makes about 3 cups (750 mL).

Pictured at right.

Directions for Sesame Snap Cookies:

Remove bag of sesame seeds from jar. Empty into small shallow bowl. Set aside. Beat 1/2 cup (125 mL) softened butter (or hard margarine), 1 large egg and 1 tsp. (5 mL) vanilla extract in large bowl. Add contents of jar. Mix well. Roll into 1 inch (2.5 cm) balls. Roll each ball in sesame seeds until coated. Arrange, about 1 inch (2.5 cm) apart, on greased cookie sheets. Flatten with fork. Bake in 325°F (160°C) oven for about 12 minutes until golden. Let stand on cookie sheets for 5 minutes before removing to wire rack to cool. Makes about 50 cookies.

1 cookie: 57 Calories; 2.8 g Total Fat (0.5 g Mono, 0.1 g Poly, 1.2 g Sat); 9 mg Cholesterol; 7 g Carbohydrate; trace Fibre; 1 g Protein; 32 mg Sodium

---

Pumpkin Pecan Loaf Mix

Whip up a batch of this dry mix and wrap it all up with a can of pumpkin and an electric mixer. This simple kit makes two good-sized loaves—the perfect treat for a young couple to enjoy as they begin their lives together.

All-purpose flour	4 cups	1 L
Granulated sugar	1 1/2 cups	375 mL
Baking powder	2 tsp.	10 mL
Ground cinnamon	1 1/2 tsp.	7 mL
Baking soda	1 tsp.	5 mL
Salt	1 tsp.	5 mL
Ground nutmeg	3/4 tsp.	4 mL
Ground cloves	1/2 tsp.	2 mL
Chopped pecans, toasted (see Tip, page 41)	1 cup	250 mL

Combine first 8 ingredients in large bowl. Spoon into jar with tight-fitting lid.

Put pecans into small resealable freezer bag. Place on top of flour mixture in jar. Makes about 6 cups (1.5 L).

Pictured at right.

Directions for Pumpkin Pecan Loaf:

Remove bag of pecans from jar. Set aside. Whisk 3 large eggs, 1 cup (250 mL) cooking oil and 14 oz. (398 mL) can of pure pumpkin (no spices) in extra-large bowl. Add pecans and contents of jar. Stir until just moistened. Spread evenly in 2 greased 9 x 5 x 3 inch (22 x 12.5 x 7.5 cm) loaf pans. Bake in 350°F (175°C) oven for about 55 minutes until wooden pick inserted in centre of loaf comes out clean. Let stand in pans for 10 minutes before removing to wire racks to cool. Makes 2 loaves. Each loaf cuts into 16 slices, for a total of 32 slices.

1 slice: 185 Calories; 10.2 g Total Fat (5.7 g Mono, 2.9 g Poly, 0.9 g Sat); 20 mg Cholesterol; 22 g Carbohydrate; 1 g Fibre; 3 g Protein; 154 mg Sodium

---

Top: Pumpkin Pecan Loaf, above
Bottom: Sesame Snap Cookie Mix, this page

Arugula Tomato Pesto

Consider pesto a kitchen staple. It can be used in sauces, as a flavour enhancer in place of salt, or added to oil and vinegar for a simple dressing. Try giving it as a gift along with Chili Focaccia Mix, at right, and a new panini maker for a special wedding gift.

Jar of sun-dried tomatoes in oil (not drained)	8 1/2 oz.	241 mL
Arugula, lightly packed	1/2 cup	125 mL
Grated Asiago cheese	1/4 cup	60 mL
Pecan pieces, toasted (see Tip, page 41)	1/4 cup	60 mL
Garlic cloves, minced	2	2

Process all 5 ingredients in food processor until smooth. Spoon into 3 sterile 1/2 cup (125 mL) jars with tight-fitting lids. Store in refrigerator for up to 2 weeks (see Note). Makes about 1 1/3 cups (325 mL).

1 tbsp. (15 mL): 84 Calories; 8.8 g Total Fat (5.7 g Mono, 1.3 g Poly, 1.4 g Sat); 1 mg Cholesterol; 2 g Carbohydrate; 1 g Fibre; 1 g Protein; 30 mg Sodium

Pictured at right.

Note: Mixture can be frozen in ice cube trays until firm, and then cubes can be transferred to resealable freezer bag.

Chili Focaccia Mix

Things are sure to be busy for those newlyweds! Help them out with a simple mix they can use to bake up some fresh focaccia bread. You could include a good bottle of olive oil and some balsamic vinegar or a jar of Arugula Tomato Pesto, at left, to complete the experience.

All-purpose flour	2 1/2 cups	625 mL
Envelope of instant yeast (or 2 1/4 tsp., 11 mL)	1/4 oz.	8 g
Ground chipotle chili pepper	1 tsp.	5 mL
Salt	1 tsp.	5 mL
Granulated sugar	1 tsp.	5 mL

Combine all 5 ingredients in medium bowl. Spoon into jar with tight-fitting lid. Makes about 2 1/2 cups (625 mL).

Pictured at right.

Directions for Chili Focaccia:

Combine contents of jar and 1/2 cup (125 mL) grated jalapeño Monterey Jack cheese in large bowl. Make a well in centre. Add 1 cup (250 mL) hot water (120°F, 51°C) and 3 tbsp. (50 mL) olive oil to well. Mix until soft dough forms. Turn out onto lightly floured surface. Knead for 5 to 10 minutes until smooth and elastic, adding additional flour 1 tbsp. (15 mL) at a time, if necessary, to prevent sticking. Transfer to greased large bowl, turning once to grease top. Cover with greased waxed paper and tea towel. Let stand in oven with light on and door closed for about 45 minutes until doubled in bulk. Punch dough down. Turn out onto lightly floured surface. Knead for 1 minute. Press evenly in greased 10 x 15 inch (25 x 38 cm) baking sheet, sprinkled with 1 tbsp. (15 mL) yellow cornmeal. Cover with greased waxed paper and tea towel. Let stand in oven with light on and door closed for about 30 minutes until doubled in size. Bake in 400°F (205°C) oven for about 15 minutes until golden. Let stand in pan for 10 minutes before removing to wire rack to cool. Cuts into 8 pieces.

1 piece: 205 Calories; 7.6 g Total Fat (3.8 g Mono, 0.8 g Poly, 2.0 g Sat); 6 mg Cholesterol; 30 g Carbohydrate; 1 g Fibre; 6 g Protein; 354 mg Sodium

Left: Arugula Tomato Pesto, this page
Right: Chili Focaccia Mix, above

Macadamia Chip Brownies

Celebrate the big move into a new house with a batch of these decadent brownies. A great treat that everyone's sure to enjoy after a hard day's labour.

Semi-sweet chocolate baking squares (1 oz., 28 g, each), coarsely chopped	2	2
Brown sugar, packed	1 cup	250 mL
All-purpose flour	2/3 cup	150 mL
Cocoa, sifted if lumpy	1/2 cup	125 mL
Salt	1/4 tsp.	1 mL
Large eggs	2	2
Applesauce	1/2 cup	125 mL
Cooking oil	2 tbsp.	30 mL
White chocolate chips	1 cup	250 mL
Chopped raw macadamia nuts, toasted (see Tip, page 41)	1/2 cup	125 mL

Line 9 x 9 inch (22 x 22 cm) pan with greased foil, leaving 1 inch (2.5 cm) overhang on 2 sides. Set aside. Put chocolate into small microwave-safe bowl. Microwave, uncovered, on medium (50%), stirring every 15 seconds, until almost melted. Stir until smooth.

Combine next 4 ingredients in medium bowl. Make a well in centre.

Whisk next 3 ingredients and melted chocolate in separate medium bowl. Add chocolate chips and macadamia nuts. Stir. Add to well. Stir until just moistened. Spread evenly in prepared pan. Bake in 350°F (175°C) oven for about 25 minutes until wooden pick inserted in centre comes out moist but not wet with batter. Do not overbake. Let stand in pan on wire rack until cool. Holding foil, remove from pan. Cuts into 36 squares.

1 square: 81 Calories; 5.2 g Total Fat (1.9 g Mono, 0.3 g Poly, 1.9 g Sat); 14 mg Cholesterol; 8 g Carbohydrate; 1 g Fibre; 2 g Protein; 76 mg Sodium

Pictured at right.

Chili Cheese Beer Bread Mix

Most people celebrate moving into a new house with beer. Why not continue with the theme with a dry mix for delicious beer bread? Chili and cheese add great flavour. Attach to a bottle of beer along with the baking directions.

Chili powder	1 tbsp.	15 mL
Parsley flakes	1 tbsp.	15 mL
Baking powder	2 tsp.	10 mL
Baking soda	1/2 tsp.	2 mL
Onion salt	1/2 tsp.	2 mL
Salt	1/2 tsp.	2 mL
Brown sugar, packed	1/4 cup	60 mL
Yellow cornmeal	1/2 cup	125 mL
Whole-wheat flour	1/2 cup	125 mL
All-purpose flour	1 cup	250 mL

Combine first 6 ingredients in small bowl. Spoon into disposable piping bag or jar with tight-fitting lid.

Layer remaining 4 ingredients, in order given, over chili mixture. Makes about 2 1/3 cups (575 mL).

Pictured at right.

Directions for Chili Cheese Beer Bread:

Combine contents of jar and 1/2 cup (125 mL) grated Parmesan cheese in medium bowl. Make a well in centre. Add 12 oz. (341 mL) bottle of honey brown ale and 2 tbsp. (30 mL) cooking oil to well. Stir until just moistened. Spread evenly in greased 9 inch (22 cm) round pan. Bake in 375°F (190°C) oven for about 28 minutes until wooden pick inserted in centre of loaf comes out clean. Let stand in pan for 5 minutes before removing to wire rack to cool. Cuts into 8 wedges.

1 wedge: 212 Calories; 6.1 g Total Fat (2.1 g Mono, 1.2 g Poly, 1.8 g Sat); 8 mg Cholesterol; 32 g Carbohydrate; 2 g Fibre; 6 g Protein; 647 mg Sodium

---

Left: Macadamia Chip Brownies, this page
Right: Chili Cheese Beer Bread Mix, above

Pineapple Buckwheat Pancake Mix

New parents are just about the busiest people you can find. Lend them a hand with a package of this delicious and nutritious pancake mix. Include a can of crushed pineapple and a bottle of Pineapple Rhubarb Syrup, at right, for a complete breakfast kit.

All-purpose flour	1 cup	250 mL
Buckwheat flour	1/3 cup	75 mL
Buttermilk powder	1/3 cup	75 mL
Granulated sugar	1 tbsp.	15 mL
Baking powder	1 tbsp.	15 mL
Salt	1/2 tsp.	2 mL
Cooking oil	2 tbsp.	30 mL

Combine first 6 ingredients in medium bowl.

Add cooking oil, in thin, steady stream, beating constantly on low, until mixture resembles coarse crumbs. Spoon into jar with tight-fitting lid. Makes about 2 1/3 cups (575 mL).

Pictured at right.

Directions for Pineapple Buckwheat Pancakes:

Empty contents of jar into medium bowl. Make a well in centre. Beat 1 large egg with fork in small bowl. Add 14 oz. (398 mL) can of crushed pineapple (with juice) and 1/4 cup (60 mL) water. Stir. Add to well. Stir until just moistened. Batter will be lumpy. Preheat griddle to medium-high. Spray with cooking spray. Reduce heat to medium. Pour batter onto griddle, using about 1/3 cup (75 mL) for each pancake. Cook for about 2 minutes until bubbles form on top and edges appear dry. Turn pancake over. Cook for about 2 minutes until golden. Remove to plate. Cover to keep warm. Repeat with remaining batter, spraying griddle with cooking spray if necessary to prevent sticking. Makes about 10 pancakes.

1 pancake: 131 Calories; 3.7 g Total Fat (1.8 g Mono, 0.9 g Poly, 0.5 g Sat); 24 mg Cholesterol; 21 g Carbohydrate; 1 g Fibre; 4 g Protein; 314 mg Sodium

---

Pineapple Rhubarb Syrup

This delicious, yet completely unexpected blend of sweet and tart flavours makes an ordinary pancake breakfast extraordinary. Try it with Pineapple Buckwheat Pancakes, at left.

Chopped fresh (or frozen) rhubarb	2 cups	500 mL
Can of crushed pineapple (with juice)	14 oz.	398 mL
Water	1/2 cup	125 mL
Salt, sprinkle		
Granulated sugar	2 2/3 cups	650 mL
Brandy (optional)	1 tbsp.	15 mL

Combine first 4 ingredients in medium saucepan. Bring to a boil, stirring constantly. Reduce heat to medium-low. Simmer, covered, for about 10 minutes until rhubarb is softened. Remove from heat. Let stand for 5 minutes. Carefully process with hand blender until smooth (see Safety Tip). Strain through fine sieve into separate medium saucepan. Discard solids.

Add sugar and brandy to fruit mixture. Stir until sugar is dissolved. Bring to a boil. Reduce heat to medium. Boil gently, uncovered, for 2 minutes, without stirring. Skim and discard foam. Pour into 5 sterile 1/2 cup (125 mL) jars with tight-fitting lids. Makes about 2 2/3 cups (650 mL).

1 tbsp (15 mL): 32 Calories; 0 g Total Fat (0 g Mono, 0 g Poly, 0 g Sat); 0 mg Cholesterol; 9 g Carbohydrate; trace Fibre; trace Protein; trace Sodium

Pictured on page 40 and at right.

Safety Tip: Follow blender manufacturer's instructions for processing hot liquids.

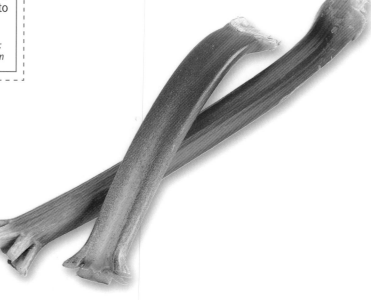

Left: Pineapple Rhubarb Syrup, above
Right: Pineapple Buckwheat Pancake Mix, this page

Mommy's Midnight Morsels

Show your thoughtfulness with this simple gift. Those new parents are bound to be up at all hours of the night as their new baby settles in. Full of concentrated energy and vitamins and low in fat, these cookies are the perfect snack to keep Mom and Dad going.

Large flake rolled oats	1 1/2 cups	375 mL
All-purpose flour	1 cup	250 mL
Whole-wheat flour	1 cup	250 mL
Baking soda	1 tsp.	5 mL
Ground cinnamon	1 tsp.	5 mL
Ground nutmeg	1/4 tsp.	1 mL
Salt	1/4 tsp.	1 mL
Ground cloves	1/8 tsp.	0.5 mL
Large eggs, fork-beaten	2	2
Applesauce	1/2 cup	125 mL
Pure pumpkin (no spices)	1/2 cup	125 mL
Vanilla extract	1 tsp.	5 mL
Butter (or hard margarine), softened	1 cup	250 mL
Brown sugar, packed	1 cup	250 mL
Chopped dried apricot	1 cup	250 mL
Dried cranberries	1 cup	250 mL
Golden raisins	1/2 cup	125 mL

Combine first 8 ingredients in large bowl. Set aside.

Combine next 4 ingredients in medium bowl.

Beat butter and brown sugar in separate large bowl until light and fluffy. Add pumpkin mixture. Beat until smooth. Add flour mixture in 2 additions, beating well after each addition until no dry flour remains.

Add remaining 3 ingredients. Stir. Drop, using 1 heaping tablespoon for each, about 1 inch (2.5 cm) apart onto greased cookie sheets. Bake in 350°F (175°C) oven for about 12 minutes until firm and golden on bottom. Let stand on cookie sheets for 5 minutes before removing to wire racks to cool. Cool cookie sheets between batches. Makes about 60 morsels.

1 morsel: 82 Calories; 3.4 g Total Fat (0.9 g Mono, 0.2 g Poly, 2.0 g Sat); 15 mg Cholesterol; 12 g Carbohydrate; 1 g Fibre; 1 g Protein; 58 mg Sodium

Pictured at right.

Fruity Power Muffins

Keep the power levels high—Mom and Dad are going to need lots of energy to keep up with the hectic schedule of a new parent. These sweet muffins are packed with all the good stuff, like sunflower seeds, pineapple and dried fruit, that they need to keep going. Using paper liners makes these muffins easy to wrap for gifting.

All-purpose flour	1 cup	250 mL
Whole-wheat flour	1 cup	250 mL
Chopped dried apricot	1/2 cup	125 mL
Dried blueberries (or raisins)	1/2 cup	125 mL
Unsalted, roasted sunflower seeds	1/2 cup	125 mL
Brown sugar, packed	2 tbsp.	30 mL
Baking soda	1 tsp.	5 mL
Ground cinnamon	1 tsp.	5 mL
Ground allspice	1/4 tsp.	1 mL
Ground ginger	1/4 tsp.	1 mL
Salt	1/4 tsp.	1 mL
Large eggs, fork-beaten	2	2
Can of crushed pineapple (with juice)	14 oz.	398 mL
Cooking oil	1/3 cup	75 mL

Combine first 11 ingredients in large bowl. Make a well in centre.

Combine remaining 3 ingredients in small bowl. Add to well. Stir until just moistened. Fill 12 paper-lined muffin cups full. Bake in 375°F (190°C) oven for about 30 minutes until wooden pick inserted in centre of muffin comes out clean. Let stand in pan for 5 minutes before removing to wire rack to cool. Makes 12 muffins.

1 muffin: 234 Calories; 10.1 g Total Fat (3.5 g Mono, 1.8 g Poly, 1.0 g Sat); 36 mg Cholesterol; 31 g Carbohydrate; 4 g Fibre; 6 g Protein; 181 mg Sodium

Pictured at right.

Left: Fruity Power Muffins, above
Right: Mommy's Midnight Morsels, this page

Brainy Instant Breakfast Mix

No student should live on pizza alone. This nutritious breakfast is full of fibre, vitamins and, most importantly—flavour! This dry mix makes the perfect addition to a student's care package.

Quick-cooking rolled oats	2 cups	500 mL
Quick-cooking rolled oats	4 cups	1 L
Brown sugar, packed	1/2 cup	125 mL
Skim milk powder	1/2 cup	125 mL
Ground allspice	1 tsp.	5 mL
Ground cinnamon	1 tsp.	5 mL
Salt	1/2 tsp.	2 mL
Chopped dried apple	1 cup	250 mL
Chopped dried papaya	1/2 cup	125 mL
Dark raisins	1/2 cup	125 mL

Process first amount of oats in blender or food processor until powdery. Transfer to large bowl.

Add next 6 ingredients. Stir. Measure 1/2 cup (125 mL) of oat mixture into 12 bags.

Combine remaining 3 ingredients in medium bowl. Stir. Add generous 2 tbsp. (30 mL) fruit mixture to each bag. Makes 12 instant breakfasts.

Pictured at right.

Directions for Brainy Instant Breakfast:

Empty contents of bag into bowl or large cup. Add 3/4 cup (175 mL) boiling water. Adjust the amount of water for a thicker or thinner porridge. Stir. Let stand, covered, for 5 minutes.

Microwave Directions for Brainy Instant Breakfast:

Empty contents of bag into microwave-safe bowl. Add 3/4 cup (175 mL) water. Stir. Cook, uncovered, on high (100%) for about 1 1/2 minutes until boiling. Stir. Let stand, uncovered, for 5 minutes.

1 instant breakfast: 297 Calories; 3.2 g Total Fat (trace Mono, trace Poly, trace Sat); 1 mg Cholesterol; 60 g Carbohydrate; 7 g Fibre; 8 g Protein; 210 mg Sodium

---

Bookworm Biscotti

A delicious dose of chocolate and peanut butter will give any student lots of energy for hitting the books. The perfect treat for those late-night cram sessions.

All-purpose flour	1 1/2 cups	375 mL
Baking powder	1 tsp.	5 mL
Salt	1/8 tsp.	0.5 mL
Butter (or hard margarine), softened	1/4 cup	60 mL
Granulated sugar	3/4 cup	175 mL
Large egg	1	1
Vanilla extract	1/2 tsp.	2 mL
Crunchy peanut butter	1/2 cup	125 mL
Mini semi-sweet chocolate chips	1/2 cup	125 mL

Combine first 3 ingredients in small bowl.

Beat butter and sugar in medium bowl until light and fluffy. Add next three ingredients. Beat well. Add flour mixture in 2 additions, beating well after each addition until no dry flour remains.

Add chocolate chips. Stir. Divide dough into 2 equal portions. Roll each portion into 10 inch (25 cm) long log. Place, about 4 inches (10 cm) apart, on greased cookie sheet. Flatten logs slightly. Bake in 350°F (175°C) oven for about 25 minutes until golden. Remove from oven. Let stand for about 10 minutes until cool enough to handle. Using serrated knife, cut each log diagonally into 1/2 inch (12 mm) slices. Arrange on greased baking sheet. Reduce heat to 300°F (150°C). Bake for about 25 minutes, turning once at halftime, until dry and crisp. Let stand on cookie sheets for about 5 minutes before removing to wire racks to cool completely. Makes about 24 biscotti.

1 biscotti: 118 Calories; 5.9 g Total Fat (2.2 g Mono, 0.9 g Poly, 2.3 g Sat); 14 mg Cholesterol; 15 g Carbohydrate; 1 g Fibre; 2 g Protein; 78 mg Sodium

Pictured at right.

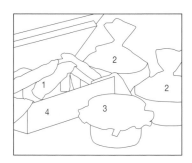

1. Bookworm Biscotti, above
2. Brainy Instant Breakfast Mix, this page
3. Sugar And Spice Cereal Seasoning, page 66
4. Book Box, right

Book Box

The perfect gift for someone you know who loves to read. Fill with Bookworm Biscotti, at left, and let your favourite bookworm settle in for a relaxing evening of reading.

MATERIALS
Paper mâché book box
Two 12 inch (30 cm) squares of cardstock
12 inch (30 cm) square of beige paper
Cording to match paper

TOOLS
ruler, pencil, paper trimmer or scissors, fast-grab tacky glue

Carefully measure the spine and inside flap of the book. Carefully measure pieces of cardstock to fit the covers and spine of the book. Cut with the paper trimmer. Glue all the pieces in place. Let dry. Repeat with the beige paper for the "pages" of the book.

Cut cording to fit along sides of spine and glue in place.

Pictured below.

Sugar and Spice Cereal Seasoning

Everyone knows that no one should skip breakfast. Ensure that kids who are away from home for the first time are eating right with this delicious cereal topping—it's sure to encourage students to eat a healthy breakfast every day. Goes great with Brainy Instant Breakfast Mix, page 64.

Raw sugar	1 cup	250 mL
Ground cinnamon	1 tsp.	5 mL
Ground ginger	1 tsp.	5 mL
Ground nutmeg	1/2 tsp.	2 mL
Ground allspice	1/4 tsp.	1 mL
Ground cloves	1/4 tsp.	1 mL

Combine all 6 ingredients in small bowl. Spoon into jar with tight-fitting lid. Makes about 1 cup (250 mL).

Pictured on page 65.

Directions for Sugar And Spice Cereal Seasoning:

Sprinkle about 1 tsp. (5 mL) over cold cereal or hot oatmeal.

1 tsp. (5 mL) seasoning: 16 Calories; trace Total Fat (0 g Mono, 0 g Poly, trace Sat); 0 mg Cholesterol; 4 g Carbohydrate; trace Fibre; trace Protein; trace Sodium

---

Mexican Corn Salsa, this page

Mexican Corn Salsa

Snacking is just a part of the student lifestyle. At least you can make sure that their snacks are nutritious too! This easy corn salsa is packed with Mexican flavour and makes a great gift alongside a bag of tortilla chips.

Chopped tomato	2 cups	500 mL
Frozen kernel corn	2 cups	500 mL
Chopped red onion	1/2 cup	125 mL
Chopped red pepper	1/2 cup	125 mL
Lemon juice	1/4 cup	60 mL
Finely chopped fresh jalapeño pepper (see Tip, at right)	2 tbsp.	30 mL
Red wine vinegar	2 tbsp.	30 mL
Cooking oil	1 tbsp.	15 mL
Chili powder	2 tsp.	10 mL
Garlic cloves, minced (or 1/2 tsp., 2 mL, powder)	2	2
Ground cumin	2 tsp.	10 mL
Granulated sugar	1 tsp.	5 mL
Salt	1/2 tsp.	2 mL
Chopped fresh cilantro or parsley (or 1 tbsp., 15 mL, dried)	1/4 cup	60 mL

Combine first 13 ingredients in large saucepan. Bring to a boil, stirring occasionally. Reduce heat to medium-low. Simmer, uncovered, for about 30 minutes, stirring often, until mixture thickens.

Add cilantro. Heat and stir for 2 minutes. Fill 3 hot sterile 1 cup (250 mL) jars to within 1/2 inch (12 mm) of top. Wipe rims. Place sterile metal lids on jars and screw on metal bands fingertip tight. Do not over-tighten. Process in boiling water bath for 20 minutes (see Note). Remove jars. Let stand at room temperature until cool. Chill after opening. Makes about 3 cups (750 mL).

1 tbsp. (15 mL): 11 Calories; 0.4 g Total Fat (0.2 g Mono, 0.1 g Poly, trace Sat); 0 mg Cholesterol; 2 g Carbohydrate; trace Fibre; trace Protein; 28 mg Sodium

Pictured at left.

Note: Processing time is for elevations 1001 to 3000 feet (306 to 915 m) above sea level. Make adjustment for elevation in your area if necessary.

Biscotti Swirl

The first day on the job doesn't need to be stressful! Assure your friend that they're not seeing double—these delicious biscotti include two colours and two flavours for the perfect coffee break snack.

CHOCOLATE DOUGH

All-purpose flour	1 cup	250 mL
Cocoa, sifted if lumpy	2 tbsp.	30 mL
Baking powder	1/2 tsp.	2 mL
Salt	1/8 tsp.	0.5 mL
Butter (or hard margarine), softened	1/4 cup	60 mL
Granulated sugar	1/2 cup	125 mL
Large egg	1	1
Vanilla extract	1/2 tsp.	2 mL

ALMOND DOUGH

All-purpose flour	1 cup	250 mL
Ground almonds, toasted (see Tip, page 41)	1/4 cup	60 mL
Baking powder	1/2 tsp.	2 mL
Salt	1/8 tsp.	0.5 mL
Butter (or hard margarine), softened	1/4 cup	60 mL
Granulated sugar	1/2 cup	125 mL
Large egg	1	1
Almond extract	1/2 tsp.	2 mL

Chocolate Dough: Combine first 4 ingredients in small bowl.

Beat butter and sugar in medium bowl until light and fluffy. Add egg and vanilla. Beat well. Add flour mixture. Stir until dough forms. Divide into 2 equal portions. Shape portions into discs.

Almond Dough: Combine first 4 ingredients in small bowl.

Beat butter and sugar in medium bowl until light and fluffy. Add egg and almond extract. Beat well. Add flour mixture. Stir until dough forms. Divide into 2 equal portions. Shape portions into discs. Roll out 1 portion of each dough on lightly floured surface to 4 x 10 inch (10 x 25 cm) rectangles. Carefully place chocolate dough over almond dough. Press down lightly. Roll up, jelly-roll style, from long side. Press seam against roll to seal. Transfer to greased baking sheet. Press down gently to flatten slightly. Repeat with remaining dough portions. Bake in 350°F (175°C) oven for about 18 minutes until edges are golden. Remove from oven. Let stand for about 10 minutes until cool enough to handle. Using serrated knife, cut diagonally into 1/2 inch (12 mm) slices. Arrange, cut-side down, on greased baking sheet. Reduce heat to 300°F (150°C). Bake for about 25 minutes, turning at halftime, until dry and crisp. Let stand on cookie sheets for 5 minutes before removing to wire racks to cool completely. Makes about 30 biscotti.

1 biscotti: 90 Calories; 3.8 g Total Fat (1.2 g Mono, 0.3 g Poly, 2.1 g Sat); 22 mg Cholesterol; 13 g Carbohydrate; trace Fibre; 1 g Protein; 64 mg Sodium

Pictured on page 69.

Tip: Hot peppers contain capsaicin in the seeds and ribs. Removing the seeds and ribs will reduce the heat. Wear rubber gloves when handling hot peppers and avoid touching your eyes. Wash your hands well afterwards.

Mini Banana Bites

Pack these moist and delicious mini-muffins in a lunch tin for a special treat that your friend can enjoy at their first day on the job. Just a small and thoughtful gesture to wish them good luck.

All-purpose flour	1 cup	250 mL
Chopped pecans	1/4 cup	60 mL
Baking powder	1/4 tsp.	1 mL
Baking soda	1/4 tsp.	1 mL
Salt	1/4 tsp.	1 mL
Large egg	1	1
Mashed overripe banana (about 1 medium)	1/2 cup	125 mL
Granulated sugar	1/3 cup	75 mL
Sour cream	1/4 cup	60 mL
Cooking oil	2 tbsp.	30 mL

Combine first 5 ingredients in medium bowl. Make a well in centre.

Combine next 5 ingredients in small bowl. Add to well. Stir until just moistened. Fill 12 paper-lined mini-muffin cups full. Bake in 375°F (190°C) oven for about 18 minutes until wooden pick inserted in centre of muffin comes out clean. Let stand in pan on wire rack for 5 minutes before removing to wire rack to cool. Makes 12 mini-muffins.

1 mini-muffin: 111 Calories; 5.0 g Total Fat (2.4 g Mono, 1.2 g Poly, 0.9 g Sat); 3 mg Cholesterol; 16 g Carbohydrate; 1 g Fibre; 2 g Protein; 88 mg Sodium

Pictured at right.

Chocolate Coffee Mix

Give along with Mini Banana Bites, at left, and Biscotti Swirl, page 67, for the perfect pick-me-up for the first day of work. This rich mocha-like beverage is the perfect hot drink for a cold day.

Skim milk powder	2 1/2 cups	625 mL
Powdered coffee whitener	1 cup	250 mL
Instant coffee granules	2/3 cup	150 mL
Chocolate milk powder	1/2 cup	125 mL
Cocoa, sifted if lumpy	1/4 cup	60 mL
Box of chocolate pudding powder, 6-serving size	1/2	1/2
Granulated sugar	2 tbsp.	30 mL
Ground cinnamon	1 1/2 tsp.	7 mL

Combine all 8 ingredients in medium bowl. Spoon mixture into 12 decorative cellophane bags. Makes about 4 cups (1 L).

Pictured at right.

Directions for Chocolate Coffee:

Pour 1 cup (250 mL) boiling water into blender. Add contents of bag. Carefully process in blender or food processor until smooth and foamy (see Safety Tip). Pour into small mug. Serves 1.

1 serving: 153 Calories; 3.3 g Total Fat (0.3 g Mono, trace Poly, 2.8 g Sat); 3 mg Cholesterol; 25 g Carbohydrate; 1 g Fibre; 6 g Protein; 115 mg Sodium

Safety Tip:

Follow blender manufacturer's instructions for processing hot liquids.

1. Mini Banana Bites, this page
2. Chocolate Coffee, above
3. Biscotti Swirl, page 67
4. Chocolate Coffee Mix, above, with Hot Chocolate Gift Package, page 160

Chewsy Dog Biscuits

Cut these dog biscuits in the shapes of things your puppy loves to chew. With rewards like these, he's sure to be a good dog every day! Perfect for the Good Dog Calendar, at right.

All-purpose flour	1 cup	250 mL
Whole-wheat flour	1 cup	250 mL
Large flake rolled oats	3/4 cup	175 mL
Dried mint leaves	1/2 cup	125 mL
Large egg, fork-beaten	1	1
Smooth peanut butter	1/2 cup	125 mL
Water	1/4 cup	60 mL

Process first 4 ingredients in food processor until oats are powdery.

Add remaining 3 ingredients. Process with on/off motion until mixture comes together. Turn out onto lightly floured surface. Shape into ball. Flatten slightly into disc. Wrap with plastic wrap. Chill for 1 hour. Discard plastic wrap. Roll out dough on lightly floured surface to about 1/4 inch (6 mm) thickness. Cut out shapes with lightly floured 2 1/2 inch (6.4 cm) cookie cutter. Roll out scraps to cut more shapes. Arrange, about 1 inch (2.5 cm) apart, on 2 greased cookie sheets. Bake on separate racks in 350°F (175°C) oven for about 20 minutes, switching positions of cookie sheets at halftime, until golden. Turn oven off. Let stand on cookie sheets in oven for about 8 hours or overnight until dry. Store in airtight container at room temperature for up to 1 week or freeze for up to 3 months. Makes about 36 biscuits.

Pictured at right.

Good Dog Calendar

Your dog will know just how good he's been when you reward him with a treat each day! It's even got an extra treat pocket for when he's been extra good. You could also use felt glue instead of sewing.

MATERIALS
9 x 12 inch (22 x 30 cm) pieces of felt, coloured cocoa, beige, pumpkin, gold, militia blue, red, hot pink and grey
Eight 4 x 3 inch (10 x 7.5 cm) pieces of black felt
Embellishments (small piece of chain, yellow and pink embroidery floss, black seed beads, lace with pearls, mini white fence, wooden dog), optional
16 x 18 inch (40 x 45 cm) sheet of stiff black felt
3-D fabric paints (black, lime green, white)
Package of foam alphabet stickers
Rope (18 inches, 45 cm, long)

TOOLS
scissors, pinking shears (optional), ruler, sewing machine, black thread, needle, felt glue

Enlarge patterns by 200%. Cut out pattern pieces. Use the pinking shears to make the bottom of the shoe look like a grip. Pin the pattern pieces to the felt colours and cut out as follows:

Cocoa: football (Pattern 1)

Beige: bone (Pattern 2)

Pumpkin: dog house (Pattern 3)

Gold: car body (Pattern 4A)

Militia blue: shoe (Pattern 5)

Red: fire hydrant (Pattern 6)

Hot pink: heart (Pattern 7)

Grey: cat (Pattern 8), car window and wheels (Patterns 4B and C)

Arrange the felt cutouts over the 4 x 3 inch (10 x 7.5 cm) pieces of felt. Sew or glue the cut outs to the squares. Before you attach the pockets to the calendar, add any embellishments that you will need to attach to the back of the pockets to secure. Sew the chain to the fire hydrant by hand. Using black thread, sew the black seed beads to the cat for eyes. Using the pink embroidery floss, sew a nose for the cat. Glue a lace collar to the cat. Using the yellow embroidery floss, make a shoelace pattern on the shoe.

Start at the bottom left corner and pin the pockets to the stiff black felt. Put each row of pockets 1/2 inch (12 mm) above the previous row. Use the sewing machine to sew each pocket in place, leaving the tops of the pockets open.

(continued on next page)

With the black 3-D paint, draw the lines on the fire hydrant and write "Super Dog" on the heart. Let dry. With the white 3-D paint, draw the lines on the football. Let dry. With the lime green 3-D paint, write the dog's name on the dog house and at the top of the calendar. Spell out the days of the week with the foam alphabet stickers and glue to the pockets. Glue the fence to the doghouse and the dog to the Super Dog pocket.

Using black thread, sew the ends of rope to the top front corners of the calendar by hand.

Pictured at right.

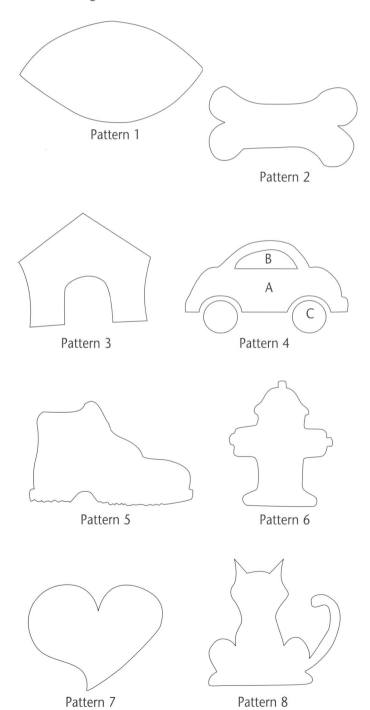

Pattern 1

Pattern 2

Pattern 3

Pattern 4

B

A

C

Pattern 5

Pattern 6

Pattern 7

Pattern 8

Good Dog Calendar, left, with Chewsy Dog Biscuits, left

Barkotti

Perfect for the pampered pet, these sophisticated treats are just what your dog deserves.

All-purpose flour	1 1/2 cups	375 mL
Whole-wheat flour	1 cup	250 mL
Yellow cornmeal	1 cup	250 mL
Finely chopped deli mild pepperoni sticks	2/3 cup	150 mL
Wheat germ	1/2 cup	125 mL
Parsley flakes	1/4 cup	60 mL
Grated Parmesan cheese	2 tbsp.	30 mL
Dried oregano	1 tbsp.	15 mL
Baking powder	1 1/2 tsp.	7 mL
Garlic powder	1 tsp.	5 mL
Large eggs	3	3
Cooking oil	1/3 cup	75 mL
Water	1/3 cup	75 mL

Combine first 10 ingredients in large bowl. Make a well in centre.

Whisk remaining 3 ingredients in medium bowl. Add to well. Stir until soft dough forms. Turn out onto lightly floured surface. Knead 6 times. Divide dough in half. Roll each half into 10 inch (25 cm) long log. Place logs on greased baking sheet, about 2 inches (5 cm) apart. Flatten logs slightly. Bake in 375°F (190°C) oven for about 25 minutes until golden. Let stand on baking sheet for about 30 minutes until cool enough to handle. Using serrated knife, cut logs diagonally into 1/2 inch (12 mm) slices. Arrange on greased baking sheet. Bake in 350°F (175°C) oven for about 25 minutes, turning at halftime, until dry and browned on bottom. Let stand on baking sheet for 5 minutes before removing to wire racks to cool completely. Store in airtight container at room temperature for up to 1 week or freeze for up to 3 months. Makes about 29 barkotti.

Pictured below.

Bow-Wow Bowl

Serve up your dog's dinner in a bowl that can be eaten too! The scraps can be rolled out and cut to make small treats for those times when an extra reward is in order.

All-purpose flour	1 cup	250 mL
Whole-wheat flour	1 cup	250 mL
Yellow cornmeal	1/2 cup	125 mL
Large eggs	2	2
Peanut butter	1/2 cup	125 mL
Water	1/4 cup	60 mL
Cooking oil	2 tbsp.	30 mL

Place 1 quart (1 L) heatproof bowl upside down on work surface. Cover outside of bowl with foil. Spray foil with cooking spray. Combine first 3 ingredients in large bowl. Make a well in centre.

Whisk remaining 4 ingredients in small bowl until combined. Add to well. Stir until dough forms. Turn out onto lightly floured surface. Roll out to 11 inch (28 cm) diameter circle, about 1/4 inch (6 mm) thick. Place dough over foil-covered bowl. Press to bowl shape. Trim excess from bottom edge. Place bowl on ungreased baking sheet. Bake in 350°F (175°C) oven for about 45 minutes until firm. Carefully invert onto wire rack. Holding foil, remove bowl. Invert baked dough onto same baking sheet. Return to oven. Turn oven off. Let stand in oven for about 30 minutes until crisp and dry. Let stand on wire rack until cool. Makes 1 bowl.

Pictured at left.

Left: Bow-Wow Bowl, right
Right: Barkotti, above

Chicken Nibbles

Show your feline friend some love with a few of these tasty little chicken treats.

Quick-cooking rolled oats	1 1/2 cups	375 mL
All-purpose flour	1/2 cup	125 mL
Prepared chicken broth	1/3 cup	75 mL
Chopped cooked chicken	1/4 cup	60 mL
Cooking oil	1/4 cup	60 mL

Process oats in blender or food processor until powdery. Transfer to medium bowl. Add flour. Stir. Make a well in centre.

Process remaining 3 ingredients in blender until smooth. Add to well. Stir until just combined. Turn out onto lightly floured surface. Roll out to 10 x 10 inch (25 x 25 cm) square. Cut into 1/2 x 1/2 inch (12 mm x 12 mm) squares. Arrange in single layer on greased cookie sheet. Bake in 350°F (175°C) oven for about 30 minutes until golden. Store in airtight container in refrigerator for up to 1 week, or freeze for up to 3 months. Makes about 150 nibbles.

Pictured below.

Kitty Kisses

You're sure to get lots of furry kisses when you make your kitty this extra-special tuna treat.

Can of flaked light tuna in water, with liquid	6 oz.	170 g
All-purpose flour	1 cup	250 mL
Yellow cornmeal	1 cup	250 mL
Water	1/3 cup	75 mL

Combine all 4 ingredients in medium bowl. Mix well. Knead 8 to 10 times in bowl. Divide into 4 equal portions. Roll portions into 16 inch (40 cm) long ropes. Cut logs into 1/4 inch (6 mm) slices. Arrange in single layer on greased cookie sheets. Bake in 350°F (175°C) oven for about 15 minutes until golden. Let stand on cookie sheets until cool. Store in airtight container in refrigerator for up to 1 week, or freeze for up to 3 months. Makes about 250 kisses.

Pictured below.

Left: Chicken Nibbles, above
Right: Kitty Kisses, above

Thank-You Gifts

Don't let that special someone's hard work go unnoticed! These little gifts make a big impact when it comes to showing your appreciation. Give a special thank you to your coach, baby sitter, bus driver or paper boy for a job well done—or return a kind gesture that someone's given you. These gifts let the recipient know that you've noticed that they go above and beyond the call of duty.

Chili Crackers, page 82

Red Lentil Soup Mix

This dry soup mix comes with an attractive layered presentation, perfect for the Carrot Piping Bag, at right. The lucky recipient of this thoughtful thank-you gift will see all the delicious ingredients you've packed into this appetizing and convenient soup mix.

Dried red split lentils	1 cup	250 mL
Dehydrated mixed vegetables	1/2 cup	125 mL
Vegetable bouillon powder	1 tbsp.	15 mL
Granulated sugar	1 tsp.	5 mL
Lemon pepper	1 tsp.	5 mL
Ground cumin	1/2 tsp.	2 mL
Salt	1/2 tsp.	2 mL
Dried basil	1/4 tsp.	1 mL
Dried oregano	1/4 tsp.	1 mL

Layer all 9 ingredients, in order given, in disposable piping bag or jar with tight-fitting lid. Makes about 1 2/3 cups (400 mL).

Pictured at right.

Directions for Red Lentil Soup:

Combine contents of jar and 5 1/2 cups (1.4 L) water in large saucepan. Bring to a boil. Reduce heat to medium-low. Simmer, uncovered, for about 45 minutes, stirring occasionally, until lentils and vegetables are soft. Makes about 5 1/2 cups (1.4 L).

1 cup (250 mL) soup: 141 Calories; 0.9 g Total Fat (0.1 g Mono, trace Poly, trace Sat); trace Cholesterol; 24 g Carbohydrate; 5 g Fibre; 10 g Protein; 844 mg Sodium

---

How To

Carrot Bag
Give a hearty soup mix, or any dry mix, in this unique and attractive packaging.

MATERIALS
Red Lentil Soup Mix, at left
12 inch (30 cm) clear disposable piping bag
Green tissue paper
Twine or ribbon

TOOLS
scissors, tall mug

Place empty piping bag inside a tall mug to hold the bag steady while you layer the soup mix. Leave the filled piping bag inside the mug until you seal the top.

Cut two 10 inch (25 cm) squares of green tissue paper. Lay one square over top of the other and rotate the top square a half turn. Push the centre of the tissue squares inside the top of the piping bag. Gather up the piping bag around the tissue. Tie with twine around the bag, making sure to catch the green tissue inside. Tie the twine in a bow.

Pictured below.

Left: Garden Herb Loaf Mix, page 76
Right: Red Lentil Soup Mix, left, with Carrot Bag, above

Cinnamon Spice Popcorn Mix

Everyone will think you're the sweetest when you show your gratitude with this sweet and spicy popcorn topping.

Icing (confectioner's) sugar	1 cup	250 mL
Ground cinnamon	4 tsp.	20 mL
Ground allspice	1 tsp.	5 mL
Ground nutmeg	1 tsp.	5 mL
Salt	1/2 tsp.	2 mL

Combine all 5 ingredients in small bowl. Spoon into jar with tight-fitting lid. Makes about 1 cup (250 mL).

Pictured below.

Directions for Cinnamon Spice Popcorn:

Spray 4 cups (1 L) popped corn with cooking spray. Sprinkle with 1 tbsp. (15 mL) mix. Toss. Spray with cooking spray. Sprinkle with another 1 tbsp. (15 mL) mix. Toss until coated. Makes about 4 cups (1L).

1 cup (250 mL) popcorn: 134 Calories; 0.8 g Total Fat (0.1 g Mono, 0.2 g Poly, 0.2 g Sat); 0 mg Cholesterol; 32 g Carbohydrate; 2 g Fibre; 1 g Protein; 234 mg Sodium

---

Cinnamon Spice Popcorn Mix, above

Garden Herb Loaf Mix

This dry mix makes a delicious loaf packed with Italian flavours of dried herbs and Parmesan cheese. Since there's nothing better than a bowl of soup with hot bread, include a package of Red Lentil Soup Mix, page 75, for a complete lunch.

All-purpose flour	2 cups	500 mL
Buttermilk powder	2 tbsp.	30 mL
Granulated sugar	2 tbsp.	30 mL
Minced onion flakes	2 tbsp.	30 mL
Baking powder	1 tbsp.	15 mL
Baking soda	1 tsp.	5 mL
Dried oregano	1 tsp.	5 mL
Dried savory	1 tsp.	5 mL
Dried marjoram	1/2 tsp.	2 mL
Salt	1/4 tsp.	1 mL
Pepper	1/4 tsp.	1 mL
Cold vegetable shortening, cut up	1/4 cup	60 mL

Process first 11 ingredients in food processor for 30 seconds.

Add shortening. Process with on/off motion until combined. Spoon into jar with tight-fitting lid. Makes about 3 1/3 cups (825 mL).

Pictured on page 75.

Directions for Garden Herb Loaf:

Combine contents of jar and 1/2 cup (125 mL) grated Parmesan cheese in large bowl. Make a well in centre. Add 1 1/2 cups (375 mL) water to well. Stir until just moistened. Spread evenly in greased 9 x 5 x 3 inch (22 x 12.5 x 7.5 cm) loaf pan. Bake in 350°F (175°C) oven for about 35 minutes until wooden pick inserted in centre of loaf comes out clean. Let stand in pan for 5 minutes before removing to wire rack to cool. Cuts into 16 slices.

1 slice: 107 Calories; 4.2 g Total Fat (1 g Mono, 0.8 g Poly, 1.5 g Sat); 4 mg Cholesterol; 14 g Carbohydrate; trace Fibre; 3 g Protein; 287 mg Sodium

---

Raspberry Marshmallow Hearts

Homemade marshmallows are easier to make than you might think—and a whole lot tastier! These pink hearts don't just show how much you appreciate the recipient—they also show your creativity. You can try other shapes and flavours of gelatin to suit any occasion.

Box of raspberry jelly powder (gelatin)	3 oz.	85 g
Envelopes of unflavoured gelatin (1/4 oz., 7 g, each), about 2 tbsp. (30 mL)	2	2
Water	3/4 cup	175 mL
Granulated sugar	2 cups	500 mL
White corn syrup	1 cup	250 mL
Water	3/4 cup	175 mL
Icing (confectioner's) sugar	1/4 cup	60 mL

Sprinkle jelly powder and gelatin over first amount of water in large bowl.

Combine next 3 ingredients in medium saucepan. Bring to a boil on medium-high, stirring constantly, until sugar is dissolved. Boil for about 10 minutes, without stirring, until mixture reaches hard ball stage (about 260°F, 127°C) on candy thermometer (see Tip, below) or until small amount dropped into very cold water forms a rigid ball that is still somewhat pliable. Beat gelatin mixture for 30 seconds. With beaters running, add sugar mixture to gelatin mixture in slow steady stream. Beat on high for about 8 minutes until ribbon of mixture dropped from spoon remains on surface for a few seconds. Spread evenly in greased 10 x 15 inch (25 x 38 cm) jelly roll pan. Let stand, uncovered, at room temperature for about 8 hours or overnight until set. Cut out hearts with 2 inch (5 cm) cookie cutter (see Note).

Put icing sugar into small shallow dish. Add 1 heart. Toss until coated. Repeat with remaining icing sugar and hearts. Store in airtight container in freezer, separating layers with parchment (not waxed) paper, dusted with icing sugar. Makes about 36 hearts.

1 heart: 82 Calories; trace Total Fat (0 g Mono, 0 g Poly, 0 g Sat); 0 mg Cholesterol; 21 g Carbohydrate; 0 g Fibre; 1 g Protein; 15 mg Sodium

Pictured on page 78.

Note: After cutting out hearts, microwave marshmallow scraps in microwave-safe bowl on high (100%) for about 45 seconds, stirring at halftime, until melted. Pour into 9 x 5 inch (22 x 12.5 cm) loaf pan. Let stand until set. Cut 6 more hearts or other shapes.

Tip: Test your candy thermometer in boiling water before each use. The thermometer should read 212°F (100°C) at sea level. Adjust recipe temperature up or down based on test results. For example, if your thermometer reads 206°F (97°C), subtract 6°F (3°C) from each temperature called for in recipe. If volume in vessel is insufficient to get an accurate thermometer reading, simply tilt the pan to cover the bottom of candy thermometer at regular intervals.

Left: Raspberry Marshmallow Hearts, page 77
Right: Hazelnut Hot Chocolate Nuggets, below

Hazelnut Hot Chocolate Nuggets

These may not be gold nuggets, but they'll let that special someone know that they're one in a million. These may look like truffles, but add a couple to a mug of hot milk and you've got the best cup of hot chocolate around.

Chocolate hazelnut spread	1 cup	250 mL
Skim milk powder	1/2 cup	125 mL
Vanilla extract	2 tsp.	10 mL
Skim milk powder	2 tbsp.	30 mL

Stir first 3 ingredients in small bowl until thick paste forms. Roll into balls, using 1 tbsp. (15 mL) for each.

Put second amount of milk powder into small shallow dish. Roll balls in milk powder until coated. Store in airtight container at room temperature for up to 3 weeks (see Note). Makes about 18 nuggets.

Pictured above.

Directions for Hazelnut Hot Chocolate:

Put 2 nuggets into mug. Add 1 cup (250 mL) hot milk. Stir until dissolved. Makes about 1 cup (250 mL).

1 cup (250 mL) hot chocolate: 271 Calories; 10.0 g Total Fat (5.1 g Mono, 1.7 g Poly, 2.9 g Sat); 16 mg Cholesterol; 32 g Carbohydrate; 1 g Fibre; 13 g Protein; 174 mg Sodium

Note: Chocolate hazelnut spread is safe at room temperature so these do not need to be refrigerated.

Soothing Green Tea Blend

This soothing blend creates a gentle, well-rounded cup of tea that is sure to have your yin and yang in perfect balance. Add a little honey if you like a sweeter tea. Ensure your spices and dried herbs are fresh for best results. A perfect addition to the Bento Gift Box, page 164.

Finely chopped dried apricot	1/2 cup	125 mL
Dried mint leaves	1/4 cup	60 mL
Whole loose green tea	1/4 cup	60 mL
Fennel seed	4 tsp.	20 mL

Arrange four 6 inch (15 cm) squares of double-layered cheesecloth on work surface. Put 2 tbsp. (30 mL) apricot, 1 tbsp. (15 mL) mint, 1 tbsp. (15 mL) green tea and 1 tsp. (5 mL) fennel seed in centre of each cheesecloth square. Draw up corners and tie with butcher's string. Makes 4 tea pouches.

Pictured below and on page 167.

Directions for Soothing Green Tea:

Put 1 tea pouch into preheated teapot. Pour 2 cups (500 mL) boiling water over pouch. Let steep for 10 minutes. Squeeze and discard tea pouch. Makes about 2 cups (500 mL).

1 cup (250 mL) tea: 0 Calories; 0.0 g Total Fat (0.0 g Mono, 0.0 g Poly, 0.0 g Sat); 0 mg Cholesterol; 0 g Carbohydrate; 0 g Fibre; 0 g Protein; 0 mg Sodium

---

Green Tea Shortbread

Green tea is a popular beverage of late—and this recipe uses this trendy flavour in a whole new way. We've included green tea in a rich shortbread for a totally modern twist on an old favourite. This shortbread isn't really suitable for mailing, so we suggest delivering this gift by hand.

All-purpose flour	3/4 cup	175 mL
Icing (confectioner's) sugar	1/4 cup	60 mL
Cornstarch	2 tbsp.	30 mL
Gunpowder green tea, crushed	1 tsp.	5 mL
Butter (or hard margarine), softened	1/2 cup	125 mL
Almond extract	1/2 tsp.	2 mL

Combine first 4 ingredients in large bowl.

Add butter and extract. Beat on low until combined. Beat on medium for about 3 minutes until light and fluffy. Spoon dough into piping bag fitted with medium star tip. Pipe 18 rosettes, about 1 1/2 inches (3.8 cm) apart, on greased cookie sheet. Bake in 350°F (175°C) oven for about 12 minutes until golden. Let stand on cookie sheet for 5 minutes before removing to wire rack to cool. Makes 18 cookies.

1 cookie: 72 Calories; 5.1 g Total Fat (1.3 g Mono, 0.2 g Poly, 3.2 g Sat); 13 mg Cholesterol; 6 g Carbohydrate; trace Fibre; 1 g Protein; 36 mg Sodium

Pictured below and on page 167.

Left: Green Tea Shortbread, above
Right: Soothing Green Tea Blend, above
With Bento Gift Box, page 164

Cranapple Almond Muffins

These moist and flavourful muffins make a thoughtful gift any time of the year. And who better to thank than the bus driver? Pack these delicious muffins into the School Bus Box, page 166, for a truly unforgettable gift.

Brown sugar, packed	1/4 cup	60 mL
Ground almonds, toasted (see Tip, page 41)	1/4 cup	60 mL
All-purpose flour	1 tbsp.	15 mL
Cold butter (or hard margarine), cut up	1 tbsp.	15 mL
All-purpose flour	2 1/3 cups	575 mL
Brown sugar, packed	1 cup	250 mL
Ground almonds, toasted (see Tip, page 41)	1/4 cup	60 mL
Baking powder	2 tsp.	10 mL
Baking soda	1/2 tsp.	2 mL
Salt	1/4 tsp.	1 mL
Large eggs, fork-beaten	2	2
Buttermilk (or soured milk, see Tip, page 128)	1 1/4 cups	300 mL
Cooking oil	2 tbsp.	30 mL
Almond extract	1/2 tsp.	2 mL
Chopped frozen (or fresh) cranberries	1 cup	250 mL
Chopped peeled tart apple (such as Granny Smith)	1 cup	250 mL

Combine first 3 ingredients in small bowl. Cut in butter until mixture resembles coarse crumbs. Set aside.

Combine next 6 ingredients in large bowl. Make a well in centre.

Combine next 4 ingredients in small bowl. Add to well. Stir until just moistened.

Add cranberries and apple. Stir. Fill 12 paper-lined muffin cups 3/4 full. Sprinkle with almond mixture. Bake in 375°F (190°C) oven for 20 to 25 minutes until wooden pick inserted in centre of muffin comes out clean. Let stand in pan for 5 minutes before removing to wire rack to cool. Makes 12 muffins.

1 muffin: 256 Calories; 6.6 g Total Fat (3.0 g Mono, 1.2 g Poly, 1.5 g Sat); 40 mg Cholesterol; 45 g Carbohydrate; 1 g Fibre; 5 g Protein; 241 mg Sodium

Pictured at right.

Mint Chocolate Chip Squares

If anyone on your gift list is a mint lover, these are just the squares you're looking for. A very simple layered square that's overloaded with delicious mint flavour.

Chocolate wafer crumbs	2 cups	500 mL
Butter (or hard margarine)	1/2 cup	125 mL
Mint extract	1/2 tsp.	2 mL
Medium sweetened coconut	1 cup	250 mL
Mint chocolate chips	1 1/2 cups	375 mL
Can of sweetened condensed milk	11 oz.	300 mL

Line 9 x 9 inch (22 x 22 cm) pan with greased foil, leaving 1 inch (2.5 cm) overhang on 2 sides. Set aside. Melt butter in medium saucepan on medium. Remove from heat. Add wafer crumbs and mint extract. Stir well. Reserve 1/4 cup (60 mL) crumb mixture in small bowl. Press remaining crumb mixture firmly in prepared pan.

Layer next 3 ingredients, in order given, over crumb mixture. Sprinkle with reserved crumb mixture. Bake in 325°F (160°C) oven for about 35 minutes until bubbly and golden brown. Let stand in pan on wire rack at least 8 hours or overnight. Holding foil, remove squares from pan. Cuts into 36 squares.

1 square: 135 Calories; 7.4 g Total Fat (1.9 g Mono, 0.5 g Poly, 4.6 g Sat); 9 mg Cholesterol; 17 g Carbohydrate; 1 g Fibre; 2 g Protein; 70 mg Sodium

Pictured at right.

Left: Cranapple Almond Muffins, this page
Right: Mint Chocolate Chip Squares, above
With School Bus Gift Box, page 166

Chili Crackers

Heat things up with crisp chili-flavoured crackers full of spicy ground chipotle pepper and jalapeño cheese. These savoury bites make a great gift companion for Bruschetta Salsa, at right.

All-purpose flour	1/2 cup	125 mL
Yellow cornmeal	1/4 cup	60 mL
Baking powder	1/2 tsp.	2 mL
Ground chipotle chili pepper	1/2 tsp.	2 mL
Salt	1/8 tsp.	0.5 mL
Grated jalapeño Monterey Jack cheese	1 cup	250 mL
Butter, softened	1/4 cup	60 mL
Milk	2 tbsp.	30 mL

Combine first 5 ingredients in medium bowl. Make a well in centre.

Beat remaining 3 ingredients in small bowl until light and creamy. Add to well. Stir until soft dough forms. Roll into 4 inch (10 cm) long log. Wrap with plastic wrap. Chill for at least 3 hours. Discard plastic wrap. Cut into 1/8 inch (3 mm) slices. Arrange, about 1/2 inch (12 mm) apart, on parchment (not waxed) paper-lined baking sheet. Bake in 300°F (150°C) oven for about 25 minutes until bottoms are golden brown. Let stand on baking sheet for 5 minutes before removing to wire rack to cool. Makes about 30 crackers.

1 cracker: 37 Calories; 2.7 g Total Fat (0.4 g Mono, 0.1 g Poly, 1.6 g Sat); 7 mg Cholesterol; 2 g Carbohydrate; trace Fibre; 1 g Protein; 67 mg Sodium

Pictured on page 74 and at right.

Bruschetta Salsa

Show your coaches just how much you appreciate all the guidance and encouragement they give the team. Packed with all the Italian flavours of bruschetta, this delicious salsa makes a perfect pairing with Chili Crackers, at left.

Can of diced tomatoes, drained	14 oz.	398 mL
Jar of roasted red peppers, drained and chopped	12 oz.	340 mL
Chopped onion	1/4 cup	60 mL
Lime juice	2 tbsp.	30 mL
Olive (or cooking) oil	2 tbsp.	30 mL
Chopped fresh parsley (or 3/4 tsp., 4 mL, flakes)	1 tbsp.	15 mL
Chopped fresh rosemary (or 1/2 tsp., 2 mL, dried, crushed)	2 tsp.	10 mL
Garlic clove, minced (or 1/4 tsp., 1 mL, powder)	1	1
Granulated sugar	1/2 tsp.	2 mL
Salt	1/4 tsp.	1 mL
Pepper	1/2 tsp.	2 mL

Combine all 11 ingredients in medium bowl. Chill, covered, for 4 hours to blend flavours. Spoon into 2 sterile 1 cup (250 mL) jars with tight-fitting lids. Store in refrigerator for up to 1 week. Makes about 2 cups (500 mL).

2 tbsp. (30 mL): 46 Calories; 1.7 g Total Fat (1.2 g Mono, 0.2 g Poly, 0.2 g Sat); 0 mg Cholesterol; 5 g Carbohydrate; trace Fibre; 1 g Protein; 304 mg Sodium

Pictured at right.

Left: Bruschetta Salsa, above
Right: Chili Crackers, this page

Texas Twist Popcorn Mix

The paperboy gets up early every morning to make sure you get the day's news on time. Reward his diligence with a deliciously spicy popcorn topping that he's sure to love.

Powdered Cheddar cheese product	1/2 cup	125 mL
Dried oregano	2 tbsp.	30 mL
Ground Ancho chili pepper	2 tbsp.	30 mL
Garlic powder	1 tbsp.	15 mL
Ground cumin	1 tbsp.	15 mL
Onion powder	1 tbsp.	15 mL
Salt	1 tbsp.	15 mL

Combine all 7 ingredients in small bowl. Spoon into 2 small resealable freezer bags. Makes about 1 cup (250 mL).

Pictured at right.

Directions for Texas Twist Popcorn:

Stir well before using. Spray 3 cups (750 mL) popped corn with cooking spray. Sprinkle with 1 tbsp. (15 mL) mix. Toss until coated. Makes about 3 cups (750 mL).

1 cup (250 mL) popcorn: 50 Calories; 1.5 g Total Fat (0.1 g Mono, 0.2 g Poly, 0.5 g Sat); 2 mg Cholesterol; 8 g Carbohydrate; 2 g Fibre; 2 g Protein; 372 mg Sodium

---

Peppermint Pretzels

If you're looking for a special holiday gift to give your paperboy, these candy-coated pretzels have just the festive flair you're looking for. The saltiness of the pretzels pairs perfectly with the sweetness of chocolate and mint.

Crushed hard peppermint candy (or candy canes)	1/2 cup	125 mL
Chocolate melting wafers	1 cup	250 mL
Small pretzels	44	44

Spread candy on sheet of waxed paper.

Put chocolate wafers into medium microwave-safe bowl. Microwave, uncovered, on medium (50%), stirring every 30 seconds, until almost melted. Stir until smooth.

Place 1 pretzel on fork. Dip into chocolate until completely coated, allowing excess to drip back into bowl. Press 1 side into candy until coated. Place, candy-side up, on waxed paper-lined baking sheet. Repeat with remaining pretzels, chocolate and candy (see Tip, page 154). Let stand until set. Makes 44 pretzels.

1 pretzel: 240 Calories; 3.3 g Total Fat (0.7 g Mono, 0.6 g Poly, 1.2 g Sat); 2 mg Cholesterol; 48 g Carbohydrate; 1 g Fibre; 5 g Protein; 872 mg Sodium

Pictured at right.

Candy Popcorn Bars

Kids love the combination of candy and popcorn. So treat the young people who make your life a little easier— perhaps the paperboy or a babysitter—to a gift that they're sure to appreciate.

Popped corn (1/3 cup, 75 mL, unpopped)	10 cups	2.5 L
Salted peanuts	1 cup	250 mL
Brown sugar, packed	1 cup	250 mL
Liquid honey	1 cup	250 mL
Mini candy-coated chocolates	1 1/2 cups	375 mL

Line 9 x 13 inch (22 x 33 cm) pan with parchment (not waxed) paper, leaving 2 inch (5 cm) overhang on 2 sides. Combine popcorn and peanuts in extra-large bowl.

Combine brown sugar and honey in small saucepan. Bring to a boil on medium, stirring often, until sugar is dissolved. Drizzle over popcorn mixture. Toss until coated. Spread evenly in prepared pan.

Sprinkle chocolates over top. Press down lightly. Let stand in pan on wire rack for about 30 minutes until cooled. Holding edges of parchment paper, remove from pan. Cut into 1 x 3 inch (2.5 x 7.5 cm) bars. Wrap with plastic wrap. Makes about 32 bars.

1 bar: 156 Calories; 5.4 g Total Fat (trace Mono, trace Poly, 2.2 g Sat); 4 mg Cholesterol; 25 g Carbohydrate; 1 g Fibre; 2 g Protein; 40 mg Sodium

Pictured at right.

Clockwise from left:
Candy Popcorn Bars, above
Peppermint Pretzels, this page
Texas Twist Popcorn Mix, this page

Hostess Gifts

The host or hostess of the evening has put in a long, hard day's work to make sure the event went off without a hitch. Show how much you appreciate the invite by letting them take a moment to relax and enjoy a homemade treat once all the hard work is done.

Triple Chocolate Cookie Mix, page 100

Chocolate Liqueur

Chocolate, vodka, vanilla and sugar—with an ingredient list like that, there's no way this gift won't be appreciated!

Granulated sugar	1 cup	250 mL
Water	1 cup	250 mL
Cocoa, sifted if lumpy	1/4 cup	60 mL
Vodka (see Tip, below)	2 cups	500 mL
Vanilla bean, halved lengthwise	1	1

Combine first 3 ingredients in small saucepan. Bring to a boil, stirring constantly. Reduce heat to medium. Boil gently for 1 minute. Remove from heat. Cool.

Pour vodka into sterile jar with tight-fitting lid. Add vanilla bean and cocoa mixture. Seal jar. Shake gently. Let stand at room temperature for 4 weeks, shaking gently once every week. Strain twice through 4 layers of cheesecloth into 4 cup (1 L) liquid measure. Discard solids. Pour into sterile jar or decorative bottle with tight-fitting lid. Makes about 3 cups (750 mL).

1 oz. (30 mL): 87 Calories; 0.1 g Total Fat (0.0 g Mono, 0.0 g Poly, 0.0 g Sat); 0 mg Cholesterol; 8 g Carbohydrate; trace Fibre; trace Protein; trace Sodium

Pictured at right.

Tip: The best quality (and most expensive) alcohol is not necessary for making flavoured liqueurs, but avoid the cheaper brands as they can be harsh and bitter.

Pink Lemonade Jellies

Make your hostess happy with a small box of these soft and refreshing candies. Perfect for a barbecue or a summer dinner party. These jellies freeze particularly well, so they're great for those last-minute invites.

Envelopes of unflavoured gelatin (1/4 oz., 7 g, each)	3	3
Water	1/2 cup	125 mL
Granulated sugar	2 cups	500 mL
Water	1 cup	250 mL
Frozen concentrated pink lemonade, thawed	3/4 cup	175 mL
Drop of red liquid food colouring	1	1
Pink sanding (decorating) sugar (see Tip, page 112)	3 tbsp.	50 mL
Berry sugar	1/3 cup	75 mL

Sprinkle gelatin over first amount of water in small bowl. Let stand for 1 minute.

Combine granulated sugar and second amount of water in medium saucepan (see Safety Tip). Heat and stir on medium-high until boiling and sugar is dissolved. Boil for about 7 minutes, without stirring, brushing sides of pan with wet pastry brush to dissolve any sugar crystals, until mixture reaches hard ball stage (about 260°F, 126°C) on candy thermometer (see Tip, page 77) or until small amount dropped into very cold water forms a rigid ball that is still somewhat pliable. Remove from heat. Add gelatin mixture. Stir until gelatin is dissolved.

Add concentrated lemonade and food colouring. Stir. Skim and discard foam. Pour into greased 8 x 8 inch (20 x 20 cm) pan. Let stand at room temperature for about 4 hours until set.

Sprinkle with sanding sugar. Invert onto work surface. Using wet knife for a cleaner cut, cut into 1 inch (2.5 cm) squares. Put berry sugar into small shallow dish. Add 1 square. Turn and press into sugar until coated. Repeat with remaining berry sugar and squares. Store in airtight container, separating layers with parchment (not waxed) paper dusted with berry sugar. Makes 64 jellies.

1 jelly: 35 Calories; trace Total Fat (0.0 g Mono, 0.0 g Poly, 0.0 g Sat); trace Cholesterol; 9 g Carbohydrate; trace Fibre; trace Protein; 1 mg Sodium

Pictured at right.

Safety Tip: Use the size of saucepan specified by the recipe. Do not use a smaller pan because the lemonade mixture will foam up once the gelatin mixture is added.

Limoncello

Like a sip of sunshine, this lemon liqueur can be made year-round thanks to the availability of lemons. It's traditionally served very cold, so store it in the freezer. Great for making spiked lemonade, this liqueur makes a great hostess gift for summer get-togethers. Make eight weeks before gifting.

Large lemons (see Tip, page 15)	8	8
Vodka, 50% alcohol (see Tip, page 87)	1 1/2 cups	375 mL
Granulated sugar	1 1/2 cups	375 mL
Water	1 cup	250 mL
Vodka, 50% alcohol (see Tip, page 87)	1 1/2 cups	375 mL

Remove rind from lemons using vegetable peeler. Put into 2 quart (2 L) jar with tight-fitting lid. Add first amount of vodka. Seal jar. Let stand at room temperature for 4 weeks.

Combine sugar and water in small saucepan. Bring to a boil, stirring constantly until sugar is dissolved. Remove from heat. Cool to room temperature. Add second amount of vodka. Stir. Add to lemon mixture. Seal jar. Let stand at room temperature for 4 weeks. Strain through double layer of cheesecloth into 8 cup (2 L) liquid measure. Discard solids. Pour into sterile jars or decorative bottles with tight-fitting lids. Makes about 4 3/4 cups (1.2 L).

1 oz. (30 mL): 78 Calories; 0.0 g Total Fat (0.0 g Mono, 0.0 g Poly, 0.0 g Sat); 0 mg Cholesterol; 8 g Carbohydrate; 0 g Fibre; 0 g Protein; trace Sodium

Pictured at right.

Left: Pink Lemonade Jellies, this page
Right: Limoncello, above

Peppercorn Mustard Vinegar

This versatile vinegar adds a big dose of flavour to salad dressings, or any other recipe that calls for flavoured vinegar. The broad appeal of this flavourful condiment makes it the perfect choice for gifting.

White wine vinegar	3/4 cup	175 mL
Water	1/4 cup	60 mL
Whole mixed peppercorns	1 1/2 tsp.	7 mL
Celery salt	1 tsp.	5 mL
Yellow mustard seed	1 tsp.	5 mL
Granulated sugar	1/2 tsp.	2 mL

Combine all 6 ingredients in medium saucepan. Bring to a boil on medium, stirring occasionally. Boil gently, uncovered, for 2 minutes. Cool completely. Strain into 1 cup (250 mL) liquid measure. Discard solids. Pour into sterile 8 oz. (227 mL) jar with tight-fitting lid. Store at room temperature for up to 3 weeks. Makes about 1 cup (250 mL).

Pictured at right.

> **Directions for Peppercorn Mustard Dressing:**
>
> Combine equal parts olive oil and Peppercorn Mustard Vinegar in jar with tight-fitting lid. Shake well. Drizzle over salad or vegetables. Toss gently.
>
> *1 tbsp. (15 mL) dressing: 115 Calories; 13.4 g Total Fat (9.6 g Mono, 1.9 g Poly, 1.9 g Sat); 0 mg Cholesterol; trace Carbohydrate; 0 g Fibre; 0 g Protein; 60 mg Sodium*

Seasoned Salt Mix

Instead of adding plain-Jane table salt to your food, use this seasoning mix to add big flavour to almost anything. Using just a few basic ingredients from your spice cupboard, this recipe can be put together quickly for a last-minute hostess gift.

Salt	1/2 cup	125 mL
Onion powder	1/4 cup	60 mL
Garlic powder	1/4 cup	60 mL
Celery salt	1 tbsp.	15 mL
Pepper	1 tbsp.	15 mL
Sweet smoked paprika	1 tbsp.	15 mL
Dry mustard	1/2 tsp.	2 mL

Combine all 7 ingredients in small bowl. Spoon into jar with tight-fitting lid. Makes about 1 cup (250 mL).

1/4 tsp. (1 mL): 1 Calorie; 0 g Total Fat (0 g Mono, 0 g Poly, 0 g Sat); 0 mg Cholesterol; trace Carbohydrate; trace Fibre; trace Protein; 235 mg Sodium

Pictured at right.

Woven Ribbon Gift Box

Why use an ordinary box to hold your gift? This fast and easy gift box doesn't take a lot of time to put together, but sure dresses up the presentation.

MATERIALS
Square box
Two different kinds of ribbon

TOOLS
scissors, glue gun

Use a piece of ribbon to measure the distance around the lid of the box. Measure from one inside edge, up around the top, and down the other side to the inside edge. This will be the size all your pieces of ribbon will need to be. Cut the number of pieces it will take to cover the width of your lid. You should have the same number of pieces for each type of ribbon.

Start on one side of the inside flap of the lid and glue on the ends of the pieces of ribbon, side-by-side. Alternate ribbons until you cover the side. Pull each ribbon, over the top of the lid to the underside of the lid and glue in place.

Repeat with more pieces of ribbon, gluing pieces to one adjacent side of the lid. Weave each piece through the other ribbons and then glue to the opposite underside (see photo).

Pictured on page 93.

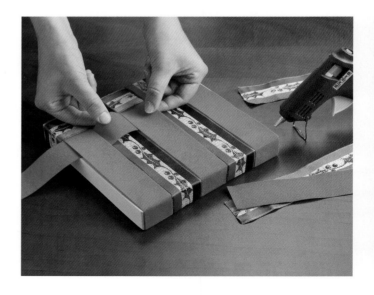

Left: Peppercorn Mustard Vinegar, this page
Right: Seasoned Salt Mix, this page

Pomegranate Delight

Spread the season's greetings with this delicious Turkish delight made from pomegranate juice. Make a big batch and store it in the freezer so you can put together a small package for anyone you might visit over the holiday season.

Granulated sugar	2 cups	500 mL
Water	1/2 cup	125 mL
Cornstarch	2/3 cup	150 mL
Cream of tartar	1/2 tsp.	2 mL
Pomegranate juice	1 cup	250 mL
Grenadine syrup	1/4 cup	60 mL
Lemon juice	1/4 cup	60 mL
Icing (confectioner's) sugar	1/4 cup	60 mL

Combine granulated sugar and water in small saucepan. Heat and stir on medium-high until boiling and sugar is dissolved. Boil for about 7 minutes, without stirring, brushing side of pan with wet pastry brush to dissolve any sugar crystals, until mixture reaches soft ball stage (235°F, 112°C) on candy thermometer (see Tip, page 77) or until small amount dropped into very cold water forms a soft ball that flattens on its own accord when removed. Remove from heat. Cover to keep warm.

Combine cornstarch and cream of tartar in separate small saucepan.

Combine next 3 ingredients in small bowl. Slowly add to cornstarch mixture, stirring constantly until smooth. Bring to a boil on medium, stirring constantly, until mixture resembles thick paste. Add sugar mixture. Reduce heat to medium-low. Cook, uncovered, for about 1 hour, stirring occasionally, until very thick and mixture pulls away from sides of pan. Transfer to well-greased parchment (not waxed) paper-lined 8 x 8 inch (20 x 20 cm) pan. Press piece of greased parchment (not waxed) paper onto surface of mixture. Press and smooth mixture evenly in pan. Discard top piece of parchment paper. Let stand, uncovered, at room temperature for about 8 hours or overnight until firm. Invert onto work surface. Cuts into 49 pieces.

Put icing sugar into small shallow bowl. Add 1 square. Turn and press into sugar until coated. Repeat with remaining sugar and squares. Store in airtight container, separating layers with parchment (not waxed) paper dusted with icing sugar. Makes about 49 pieces.

1 piece: 47 Calories; 0 g Total Fat (0 g Mono, 0 g Poly, 0 g Sat); 0 mg Cholesterol; 12 g Carbohydrate; trace Fibre; trace Protein; 1 mg Sodium

Pictured at right.

Holiday Divinity

Old-fashioned divinity gets a flavourful update with the addition of orange and cranberry. Store this super-sweet treat in the freezer for a quick Thanksgiving or Christmas gift.

Granulated sugar	3 cups	750 mL
Water	3/4 cup	175 mL
White corn syrup	3/4 cup	175 mL
Salt	1/4 tsp.	1 mL
Egg whites (large), room temperature	2	2
Box of orange jelly powder (gelatin)	3 oz.	85 g
Chopped pecans	1 cup	250 mL
Dried cranberries	1 cup	250 mL

Combine first 4 ingredients in medium saucepan. Bring to a boil on medium-high, stirring constantly. Boil for about 16 minutes, without stirring, brushing sides of pan with wet pastry brush to dissolve any sugar crystals, until mixture reaches hard ball stage (about 260°F, 127°C) on candy thermometer (see Tip, page 77) or until small amount dropped into very cold water forms a rigid ball that is still somewhat pliable.

Beat egg whites in large heatproof bowl until soft peaks form. Add jelly powder, 1 tbsp. (15 mL) at a time, beating constantly until stiff peaks form. Slowly add hot sugar mixture to egg white mixture in a thin stream, beating constantly for about 3 minutes, until mixture is very thick.

Add pecans and cranberries. Stir well. Spread evenly in parchment (not waxed) paper-lined 9 x 13 inch (22 x 33 cm) baking pan. Let stand for about 2 hours until set. Cut into 1 3/4 inch (4.5 cm) pieces. Makes about 40 pieces.

1 piece: 114 Calories; 2.2 g Total Fat (1.2 g Mono, 0.6 g Poly, 0.2 g Sat); 0 mg Cholesterol; 24 g Carbohydrate; trace Fibre; 1 g Protein; 29 mg Sodium

Pictured at right.

Left: Pomegranate Delight, this page, with Woven Ribbon Gift Box, page 90
Right: Holiday Divinity, above

Flower Bottle Topper

This is an easy and inexpensive way to brighten up a gift bottle. By using different colours of tissue paper, you can create a topper that's tops for any occasion. Here we've used red and green to make a poinsettia that's perfect for the Pom Poinsettia Sipper, at right.

MATERIALS
Two 20 x 26 inch (50 x 66 cm) sheets of green tissue paper
Two 20 x 26 inch (50 x 66 cm) sheets of red tissue paper
6 inch (15 cm) square of yellow tissue paper
Twine or string
Green ribbon

TOOLS
ruler, scissors

To make large petals, fold one sheet of green tissue paper in half and then turn and fold again. Repeat for 2 more folds until you have a rectangle, approximately 6 1/2 x 5 inches (16 x 12.5 cm). Using Diagram 1 as a guide, cut along the dotted lines. Fold the petal-shaped piece in half lengthwise. Follow Diagram 2 to make a small cut over the previous cut on the fold to make an 'X'. Repeat with 1 sheet of red tissue paper.

To make the smaller petals, fold the remaining sheet of red tissue paper until you have a 3 1/4 x 5 inch (8 x 12.5 cm) rectangle. Repeat the same cutting pattern with this rectangle.

To assemble your flower, centre the yellow tissue over the top of the bottle. Start to place the large green petals over the bottle neck. Stagger the petals as you place layers over the bottle. Do the same with the large red petals, followed by the small red petals. Include as many layers of each size or colour tissue paper as you like. The more layers you use, the fuller your flower will be.

Carefully place 1 hand over the top of the bottle to push down the centre of your flower and use your other hand to gather up the petals towards the middle. Once you have all the petals gathered, tie a piece of twine to the underside of your flower. Carefully fluff out the petals. Centre your bottle over the remaining green tissue and gather up the sides around the bottle. Tie with the ribbon.

Pictured at right and on page 159.

Pom Poinsettia Sipper

This delicious pomegranate liqueur makes a gorgeous and festive drink or an impressive gift. If you are giving it as a gift, you can decorate the bottle with a Flower Bottle Topper, at left, for added festive flair. Try adding champagne or sparkling wine for a festive sparkler.

Large ripe pomegranate	1	1
Apple juice	1 cup	250 mL
Granulated sugar	1 cup	250 mL
Water	1/2 cup	125 mL
Grated orange zest	2 tsp.	10 mL
Gin (see Tip, page 87)	1 1/2 cups	375 mL

Remove seeds from pomegranate. Discard rind and pith. Put seeds into large saucepan. Add next 4 ingredients. Bring to a boil. Reduce heat to medium-low. Simmer, uncovered, for 10 minutes to blend flavours. Remove from heat. Cool.

Add gin. Stir. Pour into 1 quart (1 L) jar with tight-fitting lid. Let stand at room temperature for 2 weeks, shaking gently every 2 days. Strain through double layer of cheesecloth into 8 cup (2 L) liquid measure. Discard solids. Pour liquid into separate jar with tight-fitting lid. Let stand at room temperature for 2 weeks. Strain through double layer of cheesecloth into 3 cup (750 mL) liquid measure. Discard solids. Pour into sterile jar or decorative bottle with tight-fitting lid. Makes about 3 cups (750 mL).

1 oz. (30 mL): 79 Calories; trace Total Fat (0 g Mono, 0 g Poly, 0 g Sat); 0 mg Cholesterol; 10 g Carbohydrate; trace Fibre; trace Protein; trace Sodium

Pictured at right.

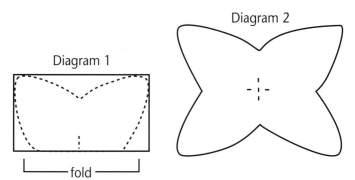

Diagram 1

Diagram 2

fold

Left: Flower Bottle Topper, this page
Right: Pom Poinsettia Sipper, above

After Midnight Mints

Ring in the new year with a chocolate mint. Elegant and classy, these pair beautifully with a cup of coffee at the end of a special meal. A great way to show the hostess of your New Year's Eve party that you appreciate all of her hard work.

Milk chocolate bars, chopped (3 1/2 oz., 100 g, each)	2	2
Butter, softened	1/3 cup	75 mL
White corn syrup	1/3 cup	75 mL
Mint extract	1/2 tsp.	2 mL
Salt	1/4 tsp.	1 mL
Icing (confectioner's) sugar	3 1/2 cups	875 mL
Dark chocolate melting wafers	3 cups	750 mL

Heat milk chocolate in small heavy saucepan on lowest heat, stirring often, until almost melted. Remove from heat. Stir until smooth.

Combine next 4 ingredients in large bowl. Add icing sugar and melted chocolate. Stir until crumbly. Knead in bowl until mixture comes together. Turn out onto work surface. Knead for about 2 minutes until smooth. Roll into 1 inch (2.5 cm) balls. Flatten into 1/2 inch (12 mm) thick patties. Arrange on waxed paper-lined baking sheets.

Heat half of chocolate wafers in small heavy saucepan (see Tip, page 12) on lowest heat, stirring often, until almost melted. Remove from heat. Stir until smooth. Place 1 patty on end of fork. Dip patty into chocolate, allowing excess to drip back into pan. Place on waxed paper-lined baking sheets. Repeat with half of remaining patties (see Tip, page 154). Add remaining chocolate wafers to saucepan. Heat on lowest heat, stirring often, until almost melted. Stir until smooth. Dip remaining patties into chocolate, allowing excess to drip back into pan. Arrange on same waxed paper-lined baking sheets. Chill for about 30 minutes until firm. Makes about 64 mint patties.

1 patty: 94 Calories; 4.4 g Total Fat (0.3 g Mono, trace Poly, 2.6 g Sat); 3 mg Cholesterol; 15 g Carbohydrate; 1 g Fibre; 1 g Protein; 22 mg Sodium

Pictured at right.

Canadiana Liqueur

The combination of Canadian whiskey and maple syrup makes for a unique and truly Canadian gift. A great gift for someone new to the country, or for a visiting relative.

Maple syrup	1 cup	250 mL
Canadian whiskey (rye), see Tip, page 87	1 cup	250 mL

Put syrup into small saucepan. Bring to a boil on medium. Boil gently for 1 minute, without stirring. Remove from heat. Cool.

Add whiskey. Stir. Pour into 2 cup (500 mL) jar with tight-fitting lid. Let stand at room temperature for 4 weeks. Pour into sterile jars or decorative bottles with tight-fitting lids. Makes about 2 cups (500 mL).

1 oz. (30 mL): 81 Calories; trace Total Fat (trace Mono, trace Poly, trace Sat); 0 mg Cholesterol; 13 g Carbohydrate; 0 g Fibre; 0 g Protein; 2 mg Sodium

Pictured at right and on page 159.

Whiskey Canadiana: Use 2/3 cup (150 mL) syrup to 1 cup (250 mL) whiskey for a stronger whiskey flavour. Makes about 1 2/3 cups (400 mL).

Left: After Midnight Mints, above
Right: Canadiana Liqueur, this page, with Bottleneck Ribbon Ring, page 158

Rustic Biscuit Mix

Thank the hostess for her hospitality by lending a helping hand in return. This handy biscuit mix, along with Strawberry Apple Jam, at right, makes a great breakfast that she and her family are sure to enjoy. This mix can be used to make either biscuits or pancakes.

All-purpose flour	1 1/2 cups	375 mL
Cake flour	2/3 cup	150 mL
Granulated sugar	2 tbsp.	30 mL
Baking powder	1 1/2 tsp.	7 mL
Salt	1/2 tsp.	2 mL
Baking soda	1/4 tsp.	1 mL
Vegetable shortening, cut up	1/4 cup	60 mL

Process first 6 ingredients in food processor for 15 seconds.

Add shortening. Process with on/off motion until mixture resembles coarse crumbs. Spoon into decorative cellophane bag or jar with tight-fitting lid. Makes about 2 2/3 cups (650 mL).

Pictured at right.

Directions for Rustic Biscuits:

Empty contents of jar into large bowl. Make a well in centre. Add 3/4 cup (175 mL) buttermilk to well. Stir until just moistened. Turn out onto work surface. Pat out to 6 inch (15 cm) circle. Transfer to greased 9 inch (22 cm) foil pie plate. Score into 8 wedges. Brush top with 1 tsp. (5 mL) milk. Bake in 425°F (220°C) oven for about 22 minutes until top is golden and wooden pick inserted in centre comes out clean. Let stand for 5 minutes. Cuts into 8 wedges.

1 wedge: 229 Calories; 8.2 g Total Fat (2.3 g Mono, 1.6 g Poly, 2.5 g Sat); 57 mg Cholesterol; 32 g Carbohydrate; 1 g Fibre; 7 g Protein; 344 mg Sodium

Directions for Rustic Pancakes:

Whisk 2 large eggs and 2 cups (500 mL) buttermilk in large bowl. Add contents of jar. Stir until just moistened. Batter will be lumpy. Preheat griddle to medium-high. Spray with cooking spray. Pour batter onto griddle, using about 1/4 cup (60 mL) for each pancake. Cook for about 3 minutes until bubbles form on top and edges appear dry. Turn pancake over. Cook for about 2 minutes until bottom is browned. Transfer to plate. Cover to keep warm. Repeat with remaining batter, spraying griddle with cooking spray between batches if necessary to prevent sticking. Makes about 15 pancakes.

1 pancake: 134 Calories; 4.8 g Total Fat (1.3 g Mono, 0.9 g Poly, 1.6 g Sat); 32 mg Cholesterol; 18 g Carbohydrate; trace Fibre; 4 g Protein; 201 mg Sodium

Strawberry Apple Jam

This traditional recipe is simply perfection. It's thickened the old-fashioned way with the natural pectin from the fruits, and the addition of brandy lends a little gift-giving flair. Sometimes the simplest things yield the most fantastic results.

Frozen (or fresh) whole strawberries, coarsely chopped	1 lb.	454 g
Coarsely chopped peeled tart apple (such as Granny Smith)	4 cups	1 L
Water	3 cups	750 mL
Lemon juice	1/4 cup	60 mL
Granulated sugar	4 cups	1 L
Brandy (optional)	1/4 cup	60 mL

Combine first 4 ingredients in Dutch oven. Bring to a boil on medium. Boil gently, uncovered, for 20 minutes, stirring occasionally.

Add sugar. Heat and stir for about 6 minutes until mixture comes to a hard boil. Boil for about 25 minutes, stirring often, until jam gels when tested on small cold plate (see Note 1). Remove from heat.

Add brandy. Stir. Fill 5 hot sterile 1 cup (250 mL) jars to within 1/4 inch (6 mm) of top. Wipe rims. Place sterile metal lids on jars and screw on metal bands fingertip tight. Do not over-tighten. Process in boiling water bath for 10 minutes (see Note 2). Remove jars. Cool. Chill after opening. Makes about 5 1/3 cups (1.3 L).

1 tbsp. (15 mL): 41 Calories; trace Total Fat (0.0 g Mono, trace Poly, 0.0 g Sat); 0 mg Cholesterol; 10 g Carbohydrate; trace Fibre; trace Protein; trace Sodium

Pictured at right.

Note 1: To make sure your jam has reached the gelling point, remove from heat, place a spoonful on a chilled plate and place it in the freezer until the mixture has reached room temperature. Press your finger down the middle of the mixture. If it doesn't run together into the groove you've created, the mixture has gelled. To prevent overcooking, don't leave the jam simmering on the stove while you're testing.

Note 2: Processing time is for elevations 1001 to 3000 feet (306 to 915 m) above sea level. Make adjustment for elevation in your area if necessary.

Left: Rustic Biscuits, this page
Right: Strawberry Apple Jam, above

Triple Chocolate Cookie Mix

This attractive cookie mix makes the perfect gift for your favourite chocoholic. These cookies include two types of chocolate chips, and they bake up moist and delicious.

Brown sugar, packed	1/2 cup	125 mL
Granulated sugar	1/2 cup	125 mL
Cocoa, sifted if lumpy	1 cup	250 mL
All-purpose flour	1 3/4 cups	425 mL
Baking soda	1/2 tsp.	2 mL
Salt	1/4 tsp.	1 mL
Semi-sweet chocolate chips	2/3 cup	150 mL
White chocolate chips	2/3 cup	150 mL

Pack brown sugar evenly in bottom of jar with tight-fitting lid. Layer granulated sugar and cocoa over top.

Combine next 3 ingredients in small bowl. Spoon over cocoa.

Layer semi-sweet and white chocolate chips over flour mixture. Makes about 4 cups (1 L).

Pictured on page 86, at right and on page 168.

Directions for Triple Chocolate Cookies:

Beat 3/4 cup (175 mL) softened butter (or hard margarine), 2 large eggs, and 1 tsp. (5 mL) vanilla extract in large bowl until smooth. Add contents of jar. Mix well. Drop, using 1 tbsp. (15 mL) for each, about 1 inch (2.5 cm) apart, onto greased cookie sheets. Bake in 375°F (190°C) oven for about 10 minutes until done. Let stand on cookie sheets for 5 minutes before removing to wire rack to cool. Cool cookie sheets between batches. Makes about 42 cookies.

1 cookie: 113 Calories; 5.9 g Total Fat (0.8 g Mono, trace Poly, 3.5 g Sat); 20 mg Cholesterol; 14 g Carbohydrate; 1 g Fibre; 2 g Protein; 60 mg Sodium

---

Caramel Pecan Fudge

Creamy caramel, crunchy pecans and chewy coconut top a smooth chocolate base. This winning combination of flavours makes for one sweet, rich fudge.

Granulated sugar	1 cup	250 mL
Butter	1/2 cup	125 mL
Golden corn syrup	1/2 cup	125 mL
Evaporated milk	1/3 cup	75 mL
Granulated sugar	2 cups	500 mL
Evaporated milk	3/4 cup	175 mL
Butter (or hard margarine)	1/2 cup	125 mL
Milk chocolate bars, chopped (3 1/2 oz., 100 g, each)	2	2
Miniature marshmallows	2 1/4 cups	550 mL
Vanilla extract	1/2 tsp.	2 mL
Chopped pecans, toasted (see Tip, page 41)	1/2 cup	125 mL
Flaked coconut	1/2 cup	125 mL

Line 9 x 9 inch (22 x 22 cm) pan with greased foil, leaving 1 inch (2.5 cm) overhang on 2 sides. Set aside. Combine first 4 ingredients in medium saucepan. Heat and stir on medium until mixture comes to a hard boil. Boil for about 4 minutes, stirring constantly, until mixture reaches soft ball stage (about 234°F, 112°C) on candy thermometer (see Tip, page 77) or until small amount dropped into very cold water forms a soft ball that flattens on its own accord when removed. Reduce heat to low. Cook, uncovered, stirring occasionally to keep warm.

Combine next 3 ingredients in large saucepan. Heat and stir on medium for about 8 minutes, until mixture reaches soft ball stage (about 234°F, 112°C) on candy thermometer or until small amount dropped into very cold water forms a soft ball that flattens on its own accord when removed. Remove from heat.

Add next 3 ingredients. Stir well. Spread evenly in prepared pan.

Remove corn syrup mixture from heat. Add pecans and coconut. Stir well. Spread evenly over chocolate mixture in pan. Let stand for about 4 hours until cool. Holding foil, remove fudge from pan. Cuts into 81 squares.

1 square: 106 Calories; 5.0 g Total Fat (1.2 g Mono, 0.3 g Poly, 2.8 g Sat); 10 mg Cholesterol; 16 g Carbohydrate; trace Fibre; 1 g Protein; 33 mg Sodium

Pictured at right and on page 168.

Left: Caramel Pecan Fudge, above
Right: Triple Chocolate Cookie Mix, this page

Favours

Why spend big money on party favours? They're easier to put together than you may think. You'll find great ideas for dinner parties, wedding favours—even baby or bridal showers. This section is packed with small gifts that go a long way. You'll even find a few fun ideas for your kids' birthday party loot bags.

White Wedding Cupcakes, page 108

Cuban Seasoning Mix

Perhaps your wedding is taking place in Cuba, or maybe your honeymoon? Continue with the Cuban theme and offer this seasoning mix as a favour at your wedding shower. Though we often associate hot spices with the Caribbean, Cuban cookery is typically more flavourful than spicy. Great for chicken or beef, or as a popcorn topping.

Dried oregano	3 tbsp.	50 mL
Ground cumin	3 tbsp.	50 mL
Paprika	3 tbsp.	50 mL
Brown sugar, packed	2 tbsp.	30 mL
Garlic powder	2 tbsp.	30 mL
Onion salt	2 tbsp.	30 mL
Salt	2 tbsp.	30 mL
Pepper	1 tbsp.	15 mL

Combine all 8 ingredients in small bowl. Spoon into jar with tight-fitting lid. Makes about 1 cup (250 mL).

Directions for Cuban Seasoning Mix:

Sprinkle over poultry, pork, beef or seafood. Let stand in refrigerator for at least 30 minutes or up to 4 hours before cooking.

1/2 tsp. (2 mL): 3 Calories; 0.1 g Total Fat (0 g Mono, trace Poly, trace Sat); 0 mg Cholesterol; 1 g Carbohydrate; trace Fibre; trace Protein; 145 mg Sodium

---

Burning Love Spice Rub

This smoky southern-style spice rub has a pleasant heat, but if you're a fan of hot food, try adding more cayenne pepper. It's great on steaks, chicken and pork. For the best results, make sure your dried herbs and spices are fragrant.

Brown sugar, packed	3/4 cup	175 mL
Minced onion flakes	1/2 cup	125 mL
Dried oregano	6 tbsp.	100 mL
Garlic powder	6 tbsp.	100 mL
Paprika	6 tbsp.	100 mL
Ground chipotle chili pepper	2 tbsp.	30 mL
Ground cumin	2 tbsp.	30 mL
Salt	2 tbsp.	30 mL
Pepper	4 1/2 tsp.	22 mL
Cayenne pepper	2 1/4 tsp.	11 mL

Combine all 10 ingredients in medium bowl. Spoon into 6 small resealable freezer bags. Seal bags. Makes about 3 cups (750 mL).

Pictured below and on page 157.

Directions for Burning Love Spice Rub:

Rub over beef, pork or poultry. Let stand in refrigerator for at least 30 minutes or up to 4 hours before cooking.

1/2 tsp. (2 mL) rub: 3 Calories; trace Total Fat (0 g Mono, trace Poly, 0 g Sat); 0 mg Cholesterol; 1 g Carbohydrate; trace Fibre; trace Protein; 38 mg Sodium

---

Burning Love Spice Rub, left

Carrot Cakes

These cute little cakes make the perfect favour for a bridal shower; they're tender and delicious with a beautiful topping of rolled fondant. Try adding Fondant Bows, at right, for an even prettier presentation. Jelly makes a perfect bonding agent for the fondant, without the hassle of another layer of icing.

All-purpose flour	2 cups	500 mL
Baking powder	2 tsp.	10 mL
Baking soda	1 tsp.	5 mL
Ground ginger	1 tsp.	5 mL
Ground cinnamon	1/2 tsp.	2 mL
Salt	1/2 tsp.	2 mL
Large eggs	4	4
Grated carrot	2 cups	500 mL
Brown sugar, packed	1 1/2 cups	375 mL
Cooking oil	1 cup	250 mL
Apple jelly, warmed	3/4 cup	175 mL
Rolled fondant	2 lbs.	900 mL

Line 10 x 15 inch (25 x 38 cm) pan with parchment paper, leaving 2 inch (5 cm) overhang on 2 sides. Set aside. Combine first 6 ingredients in large bowl. Make a well in centre.

Whisk next 3 ingredients in medium bowl until combined. Add cooking oil. Stir. Add to well. Stir until just combined. Spread evenly in prepared pan. Bake in 350°F (175°C) oven for about 25 minutes until wooden pick inserted in centre of cake comes out clean. Let stand in pan on wire rack until cooled completely. Holding parchment paper, lift cake from pan. Using serrated knife, cut into fifteen 3 x 3 inch (7.5 x 7.5 cm) squares.

Brush tops and sides with jelly.

Cut 1/4 cup (60 mL) of fondant from fondant piece. Roll out to 6 x 6 inch (15 x 15 cm) square, about 1/8 inch (3 mm) thick. Place over 1 cake square. Gently press fondant onto top and sides of cake. Trim excess along bottom edge of cake, holding sharp knife at 45° angle to work surface. Repeat with remaining fondant and cake squares. Makes 15 cakes.

1 cake: 557 Calories; 16.2 g Total Fat (8.5 g Mono, 4.3 g Poly, 1.5 g Sat); 57 mg Cholesterol; 102 g Carbohydrate; 1 g Fibre; 3 g Protein; 281 mg Sodium

Pictured at right.

Fondant Bows

Cute as can be, and much easier to make than you might think. These bows make an elegant topper for Carrot Cakes, at left. You can easily match the colour of the bows to your wedding colours with the help of paste food colourings.

Paste food colouring (see Tip, page 9)		
Rolled fondant	1 lb.	454 g
Prepared icing		
Carrot Cakes, recipe at left		

Knead food colouring into fondant until desired shade. Divide into 2 equal portions. Roll 1 portion out to 6 x 12 inch (15 x 30 cm) rectangle. Cut crosswise into twenty-four 1/2 inch (12 mm) strips. Repeat with second portion. Cut 3 strips into 1 inch (2.5 cm) pieces.

Put small dots of icing along one 6 inch (15 cm) long strip. Place, icing-side down, across centre of 1 fondant-covered cake. Press down gently. Put small dots of icing along another 6 inch (15 cm) long strip. Place, icing-side down, across first strip. Press down gently. Repeat with another 28 fondant strips and 14 cakes.

Put one 6 inch (15 cm) strip on work surface. Bring both ends up and almost to centre to form 2 loops of bow (see photo). Dampen bottom of one 1 inch (2.5 cm) fondant piece with water. Set across centre of bow. Press to seal. Repeat with remaining strips and 1 inch (2.5 cm) pieces. Let stand for about 30 minutes until dry. Put small dot of icing on bottom of each bow. Press gently onto centre of cakes. Makes 15 bows.

1 bow: 121 Calories; 0.0 g Total Fat (0.0 g Mono, 0.0 g Poly, 0.0 g Sat); 0 mg Cholesterol; 30 g Carbohydrate; 0 g Fibre; 0 g Protein; 5 mg Sodium

Pictured at right.

Apricot Orange Squares

These light, fruit-flavoured bars are a modern take on the traditional date-filled matrimonial square. The perfect favour for a wedding or a bridal shower, but you'll want to make them more often just because they're so good.

Quick-cooking rolled oats	1 1/2 cups	375 mL
All-purpose flour	1 1/4 cups	300 mL
Brown sugar, packed	1 cup	250 mL
Cold butter (or hard margarine), cut up	1 cup	250 mL
Baking soda	1 tsp.	5 mL
Dried apricots	1 1/2 cups	375 mL
Orange juice	1 1/2 cups	375 mL
Granulated sugar	1/4 cup	60 mL
Grated orange zest	1 tsp.	5 mL

Line 9 x 9 inch (22 x 22 cm) pan with greased foil, leaving 1 inch (2.5 cm) overhang on 2 sides. Set aside. Combine first 5 ingredients in food processor. Process with on/off motion until mixture resembles coarse crumbs. Press half of oat mixture in prepared pan.

Combine next 3 ingredients in small saucepan. Bring to a boil, stirring occasionally. Reduce heat to medium-low. Cook, covered, for about 15 minutes, stirring occasionally, until apricot is softened. Process in blender or food processor until almost smooth (see Safety Tip).

Add orange zest. Stir. Spread over oat mixture in pan. Sprinkle with remaining oat mixture. Press down gently. Bake in 350°F (175°C) oven for about 30 minutes until bubbly and golden brown. Let stand in pan on wire rack until cool. Holding foil, remove squares from pan. Cuts into 36 squares.

1 square: 119 Calories; 5.3 g Total Fat (1.3 g Mono, 0.2 g Poly, 3.2 g Sat); 13 mg Cholesterol; 18 g Carbohydrate; 1 g Fibre; 1 g Protein; 77 mg Sodium

Safety Tip: Follow blender manufacturer's instructions for processing hot liquids.

Fortune Cookie Favours

These charming and fun wedding favours can easily be made to match your wedding. Just use the appropriate colour of candy melting wafers and edible glitter in place of the white chocolate.

White chocolate baking squares (see Note 1), 1 oz., 28 g each, chopped	7	7
Fortune cookies	24	24
White (or coloured) edible glitter (see Note 2)	2 tbsp.	30 mL

Put chocolate into medium microwave-safe bowl (see Tip, page 12). Microwave, uncovered, on medium (50%), stirring every 30 seconds, until almost melted. Stir until smooth.

Holding both tips of fortune cookie, dip into chocolate until coated, allowing excess to drip back into bowl and leaving tips uncoated. Set cookie on waxed paper-lined baking sheet. Sprinkle with glitter. Repeat with remaining cookies, chocolate and glitter (see Tip, page 154). Chill for about 1 hour until set. Makes 24 cookies.

1 favour: 75 Calories; 2.7 g Total Fat (0 g Mono, 0 g Poly, 1.8 g Sat); 3 mg Cholesterol; 11 g Carbohydrate; trace Fibre; 1 g Protein; 12 mg Sodium

Pictured at right.

Note 1: Use 2 1/3 cups (575 mL) white candy melting wafers in place of the baking squares.

Note 2: You can buy edible glitter at stores that sell cake decorating supplies.

Fortune Cookie Favours, above

White Wedding Cupcakes

Making your own wedding favours may seem like a daunting task, especially if you're planning a big wedding. Luckily, these cupcakes can be made in advance and frozen for up to two months! Just remember that dark-coloured icings may run during thawing, so be careful if you decide to colour the buttercream.

WHITE WEDDING CUPCAKES
All-purpose flour	1 cup	250 mL
Baking powder	1 1/2 tsp.	7 mL
Salt	1/8 tsp.	0.5 mL
Butter (or hard margarine), softened	1/3 cup	75 mL
Granulated sugar	1/2 cup	125 mL
Egg whites (large)	2	2
Vanilla yogurt	1/2 cup	125 mL

VANILLA BUTTERCREAM
Milk	2 tbsp.	30 mL
Vanilla bean	1/2	1/2
Icing (confectioner's) sugar	3 cups	750 mL
Butter (or hard margarine), softened	1/2 cup	125 mL

FONDANT FLOWERS
Paste food colouring (see Tip, page 9)		
Rolled fondant	1/2 cup	125 mL

White Wedding Cupcakes: Combine first 3 ingredients in medium bowl.

Beat butter and sugar in separate medium bowl until light and creamy. Add egg whites. Beat well. Add flour mixture in 2 additions, alternating with yogurt in 1 addition, beating well after each addition until smooth. Fill 24 paper-lined mini-muffin cups 3/4 full. Bake in 350°F (175°C) oven for about 12 minutes until wooden pick inserted in centre of cupcake comes out clean. Let stand in pans for 10 minutes before removing to wire racks to cool completely.

Vanilla Buttercream: Pour milk into small cup and microwave on medium (50%) for about 1 minute. Add vanilla bean. Heat and stir on medium-low until bubbles form around edge of pan. Remove from heat. Let stand for about 5 minutes until cool. Split vanilla bean in half lengthwise. Scrape seeds from pod into milk. Discard pod.

Beat icing sugar, butter and milk mixture in large bowl for about 3 minutes until light and fluffy. Makes about 1 7/8 cup (450 mL) buttercream. Spoon into piping bag fitted with medium star tip. Pipe onto cupcakes, reserving 1 tbsp. (15 mL) buttercream in piping bag.

Fondant Flowers: Knead food colouring into fondant until desired shade. Roll out to 1/8 inch (3 mm) thickness. Cut out shapes using 1/2 inch (12 mm) flower-shaped cookie cutter. Roll out scraps to cut more shapes. Arrange flowers on waxed paper-lined baking sheet. Gently press centre of each flower with flat end of bamboo skewer or pencil tip wrapped in plastic wrap until edges of flower are raised (see Note). Pipe small dot of reserved buttercream in centre of each flower. Place flower on each cupcake. Makes 24 mini-cupcakes.

1 mini-cupcake: 170 Calories; 6.4 g Total Fat (1.6 g Mono, 0.2 g Poly, 4 g Sat); 17 mg Cholesterol; 28 g Carbohydrate; trace Fibre; 1 g Protein; 101 mg Sodium

Pictured on pages 2 and 102 and at right.

Note: The fondant flowers can be made up to 3 months in advance and stored separately in an airtight container at room temperature.

Orange Hot Chocolate Mix

This hot chocolate mix is made for all those people who dive into a box of chocolates searching for the orange-flavoured ones. Fancy up the presentation with Hot Chocolate Packages, page 160, if you're using this as a wedding favour.

Orange-flavoured chocolate bar, grated	3 1/2 oz.	100 g
Skim milk powder	1/4 cup	60 mL
Granulated sugar	2 tbsp.	30 mL

Combine all 3 ingredients in small bowl. Spoon into 4 decorative cellophane bags. Makes about 1 1/3 cups (325 mL).

Directions for Orange Hot Chocolate:

Put contents of bag into mug. Add 1 cup (250 mL) hot milk. Stir until smooth. Makes about 1 cup (250 mL).

1 cup (250 mL): 324 Calories; 9.8 g Total Fat (1.0 g Mono, 0 g Poly, 6.0 g Sat); 18 mg Cholesterol; 43 g Carbohydrate; 2 g Fibre; 15 g Protein; 218 mg Sodium

---

White Wedding Cupcakes, this page

Baby Shower Gift Bags

When your friends gather to celebrate a baby shower, send them home with these pretty bags filled with tiny treats for themselves. Try using small wrapped pieces of Dark Chocolate Almond Fudge, at right.

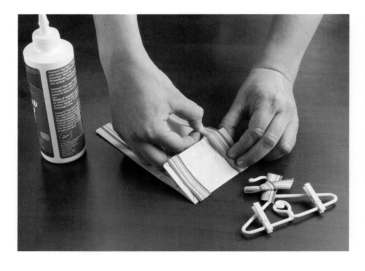

MATERIALS

3 x 5 inch (7.5 x 12.5 cm) piece of cardboard
Paper bag (3 1/4 x 2 1/4 x 6 1/2 inches, 8 x 5.5 x 16 cm)
3 x 4 inch (7.5 x 10 cm) piece of overhead transparency

Baby shower-themed embellishment
2 pieces of ribbon (15 1/2 inches, 39 cm, long), 3/8 inch
  (9 mm) wide
Piece of ribbon (9 inches, 22 cm, long)
Piece of lace (3 1/2 inches, 9 cm, long),
  3/4 inch (2 cm) wide
Doll clothes hanger (about 4 1/2 inches, 11 cm, long)
2 mini clothes pins
Small wrapped pieces of fudge or other candy

TOOLS

pencil, ruler, utility knife, eraser, tape, glue, scissors

Put cardboard inside bag as a cutting surface. Draw a 1 1/2 inch (3.8 cm) square in the centre of the seamless side of the bag, starting 1 1/4 inches (3 cm) from the bottom of the bag. Cut out the square using the ruler and utility knife. Erase any pencil marks and remove the cardboard from the bag. Put the transparency sheet into the bag behind the cut out. Tape it into place on the inside of the bag. Glue embellishment to bag above window.

Apply a small bead of glue along the wrong side of one 15 1/2 inch (39 cm) piece of ribbon. Starting at the top right side of the bag, about 1/4 inch (6 mm) in, attach ribbon down the bag, along the bottom, and around to the other side of the bag, finishing at the top. Repeat with the other piece of ribbon on the left side of the bag (see photo). Let dry.

Fold the top of the bag down 1 inch (2.5 cm) to face the side of the bag with the cut out square. Glue the lace along the top of the bag opening. Tie the 9 inch (22 cm) piece of ribbon in a bow around the neck of the hanger. Trim the ends. Put the fudge pieces into the bag. Fold the flap over and attach the hanger to the back of the bag using the 2 mini clothes pins.

Pictured at right.

Top: Baby Shower Gift Bags, left
Bottom: Dark Chocolate Almond Fudge, right

Coconut Cashew Candied Popcorn, page 112

Dark Chocolate Almond Fudge

This decadent fudge is perfect for using as a favour. With its easy preparation and great flavour, it's easy to make enough to give out—and everyone's sure to love it.

Miniature marshmallows	4 cups	1 L
Granulated sugar	1 1/2 cups	375 mL
Evaporated milk	3/4 cup	175 mL
Butter	1/4 cup	60 mL
Salt	1/4 tsp.	1 mL
Dark chocolate bars, chopped (3 1/2 oz.,100 g, each)	4	4
Chopped slivered almonds, toasted (see Tip, page 41)	2/3 cup	150 mL
Almond liqueur	1 tbsp.	15 mL

Line 9 x 9 inch (22 x 22 cm) pan with greased foil, leaving 1 inch (2.5 cm) overhang on 2 sides. Set aside. Heat and stir first 5 ingredients in large saucepan on medium until mixture comes to a hard boil. Boil for 3 minutes, stirring constantly. Remove from heat.

Add chocolate and almonds. Stir until chocolate is melted. Add liqueur. Stir. Spread evenly in prepared pan. Let stand at room temperature until set. Holding foil, remove fudge from pan. Cuts into 36 squares.

1 square: 158 Calories; 7.0 g Total Fat (1.2 g Mono, 0.4 g Poly, 3.9 g Sat); 7 mg Cholesterol; 23 g Carbohydrate; 1 g Fibre; 2 g Protein; 39 mg Sodium

Pictured at left.

Coconut Cashew Candied Popcorn

Popcorn with a satisfying crunch and just the right combination of sweet and salty. This is one treat that's definitely got a tropical twist!

Popped corn (about 1/4 cup, 60 mL, unpopped)	8 cups	2 L
Salted cashews, coarsely chopped	2 cups	500 mL
Flaked coconut, toasted (see Tip, page 41)	3/4 cup	175 mL
Brown sugar, packed	1 1/2 cups	375 mL
Butter	3/4 cup	175 mL
White corn syrup	6 tbsp.	100 mL
Baking soda	1/2 tsp.	2 mL
Salt	1/2 tsp.	2 mL
Vanilla extract	1/2 tsp.	2 mL

Combine first 3 ingredients in large bowl. Set aside.

Combine next 3 ingredients in medium saucepan. Heat and stir on medium-high until sugar is dissolved and butter is melted. Remove from heat.

Combine remaining 3 ingredients in small cup. Add to butter mixture. Stir. Pour over popped corn mixture. Stir with wooden spoon until coated. Spread evenly in greased large baking sheet with sides. Bake in 250°F (120°C) oven, stirring every 15 minutes, for 1 hour. Cool completely. Popcorn will crisp as it cools. Makes about 10 cups (2.5 L).

1 cup (250 mL): 524 Calories; 31.7 g Total Fat (3.7 g Mono, 0.7 g Poly, 13.5 g Sat); 36 mg Cholesterol; 57 g Carbohydrate; 2 g Fibre; 6 g Protein; 514 mg Sodium

Pictured on page 111.

Teddy Bear Cookies

So cute you may not want to eat them, but they taste so good you won't be able to resist! Use the same-sized cookie cutter to make Teddy Bear Tags, at right, for a cute and personalized baby shower favour.

All-purpose flour	2 1/2 cups	625 mL
Ground nutmeg	1/4 tsp.	1 mL
Salt	1/4 tsp.	1 mL
Butter (or hard margarine), softened	1 cup	250 mL
Granulated sugar	1 cup	250 mL
Large eggs	2	2
Vanilla extract	1 tbsp.	15 mL
Egg white (large), fork-beaten	1	1
Pink or blue sanding (decorating) sugar (see Tip, below)	1/4 cup	60 mL

Combine first 3 ingredients in medium bowl.

Beat butter and sugar in large bowl until light and fluffy. Add eggs and vanilla. Beat well. Add flour mixture in 2 additions, mixing well after each addition until no dry flour remains. Shape into disc. Wrap with plastic wrap. Chill for at least 3 hours. Discard plastic wrap. Roll out dough on lightly floured surface to 1/4 inch (6 mm) thickness. Cut out shapes with lightly floured 3 1/2 inch (9 cm) teddy bear-shaped cookie cutter. Roll out scraps to cut more teddy bear shapes. Arrange about 1 inch (2.5 cm) apart on parchment (not waxed) paper-lined cookie sheets.

Brush with egg white. Sprinkle with sanding sugar. Bake in 350°F (175°C) oven for about 12 minutes until edges start to turn golden. Let stand on cookie sheets for 5 minutes before removing to wire rack to cool. Cool cookie sheets between batches. Makes about 30 cookies.

1 cookie: 127 Calories; 6.4 g Total Fat (1.6 g Mono, 0.2 g Poly, 3.9 g Sat); 30 mg Cholesterol; 16 g Carbohydrate; trace Fibre; 2 g Protein; 69 mg Sodium

Pictured at right.

Tip: Sanding sugar is a coarse decorating sugar that comes in white and various colours and is available at specialty kitchen stores.

How To

Teddy Bear Tags

This project can be done in any colour to match the colours of your baby shower. For best results, use the same cookie cutter to trace the tags as you used to make the cookies.

MATERIALS
Three 12 inch (30 cm) squares of cardstock
Ink pad
1/2 inch (12 mm) letter stamp
24 Teddy Bear Cookies, at left
12 clear plastic bags (4 x 6 inches, 10 x 15 cm, each)
12 pieces of ribbon (1/4 inch, 6 mm, wide), 8 inches
 (20 cm) long
12 buttons, no larger than 1 inch (2.5 cm)

TOOLS
pencil, teddy bear cookie cutter, scissors, fine black marker,
 fast-grab tacky glue, glue gun

Using the cookie cutter, trace 12 teddy bears on the cardstock and cut out. Cut 24 strips (1 x 3 inches, 2.5 x 7.5 cm, each). Use the Patterns 1 and 2 to cut 12 small circles and 12 small hearts from the same colour cardstock.

Decorate the bears with the stamp, ink and marker. Glue 1 circle to each bear as a nose. Glue hearts onto bears' stomachs.

Fold 1/2 inch (12 mm) tab at 1 end of each paper strip. Using the glue gun, attach the tab-sides of 2 strips to the back of the bear's body on opposite sides. Place 2 cookies, back-to-back, in a clear bag and tie with ribbon. Wrap strips around cookies and glue strips together. Glue a button at the seam to finish.

Pictured at right.

Pattern 1

Pattern 2

Teddy Bear Cookies, page 112, with Teddy Bear Tags, page 113

Sparkling Play Dough

Who ever knows what to put in the loot bags at kids' birthday parties? You don't want to stuff them with candy alone! This simple recipe makes a special play dough, packed with sparkles that the kids will love. Not recommended for children under three.

All-purpose flour	1 cup	250 mL
Water	1 cup	250 mL
Salt	1/3 cup	75 mL
Cooking oil	1 tbsp.	15 mL
Cream of tartar	1 tbsp.	15 mL
Package of unsweetened drink powder	1/5 – 1/4 oz.	6 – 8 g
Fine glitter	1 tbsp.	15 mL

Combine first 6 ingredients in medium saucepan. Heat and stir on medium for about 4 minutes until mixture pulls away from sides of pan to form soft dough. Remove from heat. Let stand for about 5 minutes until cool enough to handle.

Turn out dough onto lightly greased surface. Flatten slightly. Sprinkle glitter over top. Press down lightly. Fold dough in half to enclose glitter. Knead for 1 to 2 minutes until evenly combined and dough is soft and pliable. Store in resealable bag or airtight container in refrigerator for about 2 weeks. Makes about 1 2/3 cups (400 mL).

Pictured at right.

Variations:

GLOWING GOO: Lemon-lime-flavoured drink powder with dark green glitter

MAGICIAN'S MATTER: Grape-flavoured drink powder with blue glitter

PRINCESS PUTTY: Strawberry-flavoured drink powder with silver glitter

MARTIAN MUSH: Orange-flavoured drink powder with green glitter

SUPERHERO SUBSTANCE: Blue raspberry-flavoured drink powder with red and gold glitter

GLAMOUR GIRL GUNK: Cherry-flavoured drink powder with purple and pink glitter

Cookie Creations

These cute cookies make an excellent addition to a birthday loot bag. The recipe is simple enough that you can have your kids help you prepare them.

All-purpose flour	2 1/2 cups	625 mL
Baking powder	1 tsp.	5 mL
Baking soda	1/2 tsp.	2 mL
Salt	1/8 tsp.	0.5 mL
Butter (or hard margarine), softened	1 cup	250 mL
Brown sugar, packed	1/2 cup	125 mL
Granulated sugar	1/2 cup	125 mL
Large egg	1	1
Vanilla extract	1 tsp.	5 mL
Mini candy-coated chocolates	1 1/2 cups	375 mL

Combine first 4 ingredients in small bowl.

Beat next 3 ingredients in large bowl until light and fluffy. Add egg and vanilla. Beat well. Add flour mixture in 2 additions, mixing well after each addition until no dry flour remains.

Add chocolates. Stir. Shape dough into 1 1/2 inch (3.8 cm) balls. Arrange, 2 inches (5 cm) apart, on greased cookie sheets. Flatten slightly with fork. Bake in 350°F (175°C) oven for about 10 minutes until bottoms are golden. Let stand on cookie sheets for 5 minutes before removing to wire rack to cool. Cool cookie sheets between batches. Makes about 40 cookies.

1 cookie: 130 Calories; 6.8 g Total Fat (1.2 g Mono, 0.2 g Poly, 4.1 g Sat); 20 mg Cholesterol; 17 g Carbohydrate; trace Fibre; 2 g Protein; 78 mg Sodium

Pictured at right.

Top: Birthday Loot Bag, page 162
Centre: Sparkling Play Dough, this page
Bottom: Cookie Creations, above

Raspberry Truffles

Fresh berries are a wonderful taste of summer. This recipe uses raspberry liqueur to impart a subtle raspberry flavour to velvety-smooth, creamy chocolate truffles. An excellent choice for a spring-themed dinner party.

Dark chocolate bars, chopped (3 1/2 oz., 100 g, each)	2	2
Whipping cream	1/4 cup	60 mL
Butter (or hard margarine)	1 tbsp.	15 mL
White corn syrup	1 tbsp.	15 mL
Raspberry liqueur	2 tbsp.	30 mL
White candy melting wafers	1 cup	250 mL
Dark chocolate melting wafers	1/2 cup	125 mL

Heat first 4 ingredients in small heavy saucepan on lowest heat, stirring often, until chocolate is almost melted. Remove from heat. Stir until smooth.

Add liqueur. Stir. Pour into 2 quart (2 L) baking dish. Chill, covered, for about 1 hour until firm. Roll into 1 1/2 inch (3.8 cm) egg-shaped balls, using 2 tsp. (10 mL) for each. Arrange on waxed paper-lined baking sheet. Chill for about 30 minutes until set.

Put candy wafers into small microwave-safe cup (see Tip, page 12). Microwave, uncovered, on medium (50%), stirring every 30 seconds, until almost melted. Stir until smooth. Place 1 ball on end of wooden pick. Dip into melted wafers, allowing excess to drip back into cup. Place on same waxed paper-lined baking sheet. Remove wooden pick. Repeat with remaining balls and melted wafers (see Tip, page 154).

Put chocolate wafers into separate microwave-safe small cup. Microwave, uncovered, on medium (50%), stirring every 15 seconds, until almost melted. Stir until smooth. Spoon into small piping bag fitted with smallest tip or into a resealable bag with a corner snipped off. Drizzle decorative pattern over each egg. Let stand until set. Makes about 24 truffles.

1 truffle: 124 Calories; 7.8 g Total Fat (1.2 g Mono, 0.1 g Poly, 4.8 g Sat); 6 mg Cholesterol; 13 g Carbohydrate; 1 g Fibre; 1 g Protein; 14 mg Sodium

Pictured above.

Summer Herb Dressing

Try serving this dressing of fresh herbs over a mixture of summer greens, fresh tomato and bocconcini at your next dinner party. You can send a small bottle home with your guests as a dinner favour so they can enjoy it again. If your green olives include red pimientos, be sure to remove them to keep the beautiful green colour of the dressing.

Canned navy beans, rinsed and drained	1 cup	250 mL
Cooking oil	1 cup	250 mL
Chopped large pitted green olives	1/2 cup	125 mL
Grated Parmesan cheese	1/2 cup	125 mL
White balsamic vinegar	1/2 cup	125 mL
Chopped fresh basil	1/4 cup	60 mL
Chopped fresh chives	2 tbsp.	30 mL
Chopped fresh mint	2 tbsp.	30 mL
Granulated sugar	1 1/2 tbsp.	25 mL
Salt	1/4 tsp.	1 mL
Pepper	1/4 tsp.	1 mL

Process all 11 ingredients in blender or food processor until smooth. Pour into 3 sterile 1 cup (250 mL) bottles or jars with tight-fitting lids. Store in refrigerator for up to 2 weeks. Makes about 3 cups (750 mL).

Pictured below and on page 159.

Directions for Summer Herb Dressing:

Shake well before using.

1 tbsp. (15 mL): 56 Calories; 5.2 g Total Fat (2.8 g Mono, 1.4 g Poly, 0.6 g Sat); 1 mg Cholesterol; 2 g Carbohydrate; trace Fibre; 1 g Protein; 95 mg Sodium

Apple Brandy Mustard

Celebrate the fall apple harvest with this sweet and spicy mustard. Works great as a dip for pretzels or as a spread on your favourite sandwich. You can even add it to roasted vegetables for some extra flavour.

Apple brandy	1 1/4 cups	300 mL
Apple cider vinegar	1 1/4 cups	300 mL
Brown mustard seed	2/3 cup	150 mL
Yellow mustard seed	2/3 cup	150 mL
Brown sugar, packed	1/3 cup	75 mL
Ground allspice	1/2 tsp.	2 mL
Ground ginger	1/2 tsp.	2 mL
Salt	1/2 tsp.	2 mL
Ground nutmeg	1/4 tsp.	1 mL
Ground turmeric	1/4 tsp.	1 mL

Combine first 4 ingredients in 1 quart (1 L) jar with tight-fitting lid. Let stand at room temperature for 48 hours, stirring occasionally.

Pour vinegar mixture into blender. Add remaining 6 ingredients. Process for about 3 minutes until thick and creamy. Fill 6 sterile 1/2 cup (125 mL) jars with tight-fitting lids. Let stand for at least 1 week at room temperature to let flavours develop. Makes about 3 cups (750 mL).

1 tsp. (5 mL): 13 Calories; 0.4 g Total Fat (0.1 g Mono, trace Poly, trace Sat); 0 mg Cholesterol; 2 g Carbohydrate; trace Fibre; trace Protein; 9 mg Sodium

Pictured above.

Tip: When a recipe calls for grated lemon zest and juice, it's easier to grate the lemon first, then juice it. Be careful not to grate down to the pith (white part of the peel), which is bitter and best avoided.

Tiny Tim Plum Puddings

Treat your dinner guests to a traditional holiday treat with a favour they won't soon forget. These tiny plum puddings include apricots, cranberries and orange-flavoured liqueur for a modern take on tradition, and your guests will love the presentation. Great served with ice cream.

Brandy	1/2 cup	125 mL
Chopped dried apricot	1/4 cup	60 mL
Chopped dried fig	1/4 cup	60 mL
Chopped pitted prunes	1/4 cup	60 mL
Diced mixed peel	1/4 cup	60 mL
Dried cranberries	1/4 cup	60 mL
Golden raisins	1/4 cup	60 mL
Ground allspice	1/2 tsp.	2 mL
Ground cinnamon	1/2 tsp.	2 mL
Ground ginger	1/2 tsp.	2 mL
Ground nutmeg	1/4 tsp.	1 mL
Salt	1/4 tsp.	1 mL
Ground cloves, sprinkle		
Fine dry bread crumbs	1 cup	250 mL
Orange juice	1/4 cup	60 mL
Orange liqueur	1/4 cup	60 mL
Grated orange zest (see Tip, at left)	2 tsp.	10 mL
Softened vegetable shortening	1/4 cup	60 mL
Brown sugar, packed	1/4 cup	60 mL
Large eggs, fork beaten	3	3
Cocoa, sifted if lumpy	2 tbsp.	30 mL
Orange liqueur	2 tbsp.	30 mL

Combine first 13 ingredients in large bowl. Chill, covered, for at least 8 hours or overnight, stirring occasionally.

Combine next 4 ingredients in small bowl. Let stand for about 30 minutes until crumbs are softened.

Beat shortening and brown sugar in large bowl until combined. Add eggs and cocoa. Beat well. Add bread crumb mixture. Stir. Add fruit mixture. Stir well. Spoon into 8 well-greased muffin cups. Place muffin pan in 11 x 17 inch (28 x 43 cm) baking pan. Pour boiling water into baking pan until halfway up sides of muffin cups (see Note 1). Cover with foil. Bake in 300°F (150°C) oven for about 1 hour until puddings are firm and wooden pick inserted in centre comes out clean. Remove foil. Turn oven off. Let stand in oven for 20 minutes.

Brush with half of second amount of orange liqueur. Let stand in pan on wire rack for 20 minutes before removing to wire rack to cool. Brush with remaining orange liqueur. Cool completely. Wrap in plastic wrap (see Note 2). Makes 8 plum puddings.

Pictured at right.

Note 1: Add the water to the baking pan when the muffin tin has already been placed on the oven rack.

Note 2: These cakes can be made in advance and stored in the refrigerator for up to 1 month, or in the freezer for up to 2 months.

Reheating Directions for Tiny Tim Plum Pudding:

To reheat in the oven, discard plastic wrap, wrap pudding in foil and bake in 300°F (150°C) oven for about 30 minutes until heated through. Serve warm. To reheat in the microwave, discard plastic wrap and place pudding in small microwave-safe dish. Microwave, covered, on medium (50%) for about 1 minute until heated through. Serve warm.

1 pudding: 316 Calories; 8.8 g Total Fat (2.0 g Mono, 1.5 g Poly, 2.1 g Sat); 81 mg Cholesterol; 42 g Carbohydrate; 3 g Fibre; 5 g Protein; 211 mg Sodium

Warming Mulling Spices

Serve a batch of this warm, comforting drink at your holiday dinner party, and be sure to make enough so that you can send a little of the dry mix home with each guest to enjoy on a cold winter's evening. The dry mix is perfect for packing into the Snowball Centrepiece Dinner Favours, at left.

Grated orange zest	1 1/2 tsp.	7 mL
Cinnamon sticks (4 inches, 10 cm, each), broken up	16	16
Star anise	12	12
Whole allspice	2 tbsp.	30 mL
Whole cloves	2 tbsp.	30 mL
Whole green cardamom, bruised (see Tip, this page)	12	12
Minced crystallized ginger	1 tbsp.	15 mL
Ground nutmeg	2 tsp.	10 mL

Spread orange zest evenly in greased 9 x 9 (23 x 23 cm) baking dish with sides. Bake in 200°F (95°C) oven for about 15 minutes until dry. Put into small bowl.

Add remaining 7 ingredients. Stir. Spoon into 6 small resealable freezer or decorative bags. Makes about 1 1/4 cups (300 mL).

Pictured at right.

Directions for Warming Mulled Cider:

Combine contents of bag and 8 cups (2 L) apple juice in medium saucepan. Bring to a boil. Reduce heat to medium-low. Simmer, uncovered, for 20 minutes to blend flavours. Strain through sieve into heatproof pitcher. Discard solids. Serve warm. Makes about 7 cups (1.75 L).

1 cup (250 mL) cider: 269 Calories; 0.2 g Total Fat (trace Mono, 0.0 g Poly, 0.2 g Sat); 0 mg Cholesterol; 70 g Carbohydrate; trace Fibre; trace Protein; trace Sodium

---

Snowball Centrepiece Dinner Favours

This makes six fancy favours to arrange in a nice bowl in the centre of your dinner table. Each guest gets to take one home at the end of the evening, so you may need to multiply the number of favours so no one is left out. Fill them with some of the spice blend for the cider that you've served at the party so guests can enjoy the memory of a pleasant holiday evening once they've gone home.

MATERIALS
6 acrylic balls (two piece), 3 1/4 inch (8 cm) diameter
2 jars of Snow-Tex (4 oz., 114 mL)
6 bags of Warming Mulling Spices, at left
6 pieces of ribbon or fibre (22 inches, 56 cm, long)
6 copies of recipe directions tag for Warming Mulling Spices, at left

TOOLS
small spreading knife

Take apart each ball to make 12 halves. Spread Snow-Tex over the outsides of each piece. Make sure not to get any in the track that fastens the halves together. Let dry.

Put 1 bag of mulling spices into each ball and close. Tie a piece of ribbon or fibre around the centre seam of the ball. Attach the recipe directions tag to the ribbon.

Pictured at right.

Tip: To bruise cardamom, pound pods with mallet or press with flat side of wide knife to "bruise," or crack them open slightly.

Snowball Centrepiece Dinner Favours, above, with Warming Mulling Spices, this page

Helping Hands

For those times when you want to show someone just how much you care, these homemade kitchen gifts are like giving a warm, comforting hug. Show your support when a friend or family member is coping with grief or struggling through one of life's challenges. These thoughtful gifts are made to add a touch of comfort to the lives of those in need of a helping hand.

Cheddar Bacon Cornbread, page 128

Chicken in Sun-Dried Tomato Sauce

Reminiscent of chicken cacciatore, this casserole is a dish that will please everyone. Package it with a loaf of garlic bread, some pasta or rice and a Caesar salad kit for the full-meal-deal.

All-purpose flour	1/3 cup	75 mL
Dried basil	1/4 tsp.	1 mL
Salt	1/4 tsp.	1 mL
Pepper	1/4 tsp.	1 mL
Bone-in chicken thighs, skin removed (5 – 6 oz., 140 – 170 g, each)	8	8
Olive (or cooking) oil	2 tbsp.	30 mL
Sliced onion	1 cup	250 mL
Garlic clove, minced (or 1/4 tsp., 1 mL, powder)	1	1
Dry (or alcohol-free) white wine	1/4 cup	60 mL
Can of diced tomatoes (with juice)	28 oz.	796 mL
Sliced green pepper	1 cup	250 mL
Sun-dried tomato pesto	1/3 cup	75 mL
White balsamic vinegar (or white wine vinegar)	2 tbsp.	30 mL

Combine first 4 ingredients in shallow bowl. Press chicken into flour mixture until coated. Reserve remaining flour mixture.

Heat olive oil in Dutch oven on medium-high. Add chicken. Cook for about 4 minutes per side until browned. Transfer to large plate. Reduce heat to medium.

Add onion and garlic to same pan. Cook for about 4 minutes, stirring often, until onion is softened. Add reserved flour mixture. Heat and stir for 1 minute.

Add wine. Stir. Add remaining 4 ingredients and chicken. Stir. Bring to a boil. Reduce heat to medium-low. Cook, covered, for about 20 minutes until chicken is fully cooked and internal temperature reaches 170°F (77°C). Transfer to 2 quart (2 L) foil pan. Let stand until cool. Store, covered, in refrigerator for up to 3 days. Makes about 6 1/2 cups (1.6 L).

Pictured below.

Directions for reheating Chicken in Sun-Dried Tomato Sauce:

Bake, covered, in 350°F (175°C) oven for about 75 minutes until chicken is heated through. Serves 4.

1 serving: 488 Calories; 23.5 g Total Fat (11.3 g Mono, 4.8 g Poly, 5.6 g Sat); 143 mg Cholesterol; 24 g Carbohydrate; 1 g Fibre; 43 g Protein; 1034 mg Sodium

I Love Ya Lasagna

There are layers and layers of love in this hearty lasagna—just the right kind of comfort food. Once cold, it easily cuts into portions that can be reheated for a quick and nutritious meal for someone going through challenging times.

TOMATO FENNEL MEAT SAUCE

Olive (or cooking) oil	1 tsp.	5 mL
Lean ground beef	1/2 lb.	225 g
Lean ground pork	1/2 lb.	225 g
Garlic cloves, minced	2	2
(or 1/2 tsp., 2 mL, powder)		
Fennel seed	1 tsp.	5 mL
Pepper	1/4 tsp.	1 mL
Tomato sauce	4 cups	1 L

BASIL PARMESAN CREAM SAUCE

Butter (or hard margarine)	2 tbsp.	30 mL
All-purpose flour	3 tbsp.	50 mL
Milk	3 cups	750 mL
Grated Parmesan cheese	3/4 cup	175 mL
Chopped fresh basil	1/4 cup	60 mL
(or 1 tbsp., 15 mL, dried)		
Oven-ready lasagna noodles	12	12
Grated part-skim mozzarella cheese	2 cups	500 mL
Grated Italian cheese blend	1 cup	250 mL

Tomato Fennel Meat Sauce: Heat olive oil in Dutch oven on medium-high. Add next 5 ingredients. Scramble-fry for about 7 minutes until browned.

Add tomato sauce. Stir.

Basil Parmesan Cream Sauce: Melt butter in large saucepan on medium. Add flour. Heat and stir for 1 minute. Slowly add 1/3 of milk, stirring constantly until smooth. Heat and stir until boiling and thickened. Remove from heat. Add remaining milk. Add Parmesan cheese and basil. Stir.

To assemble, layer ingredients in greased 9 x 13 inch (22 x 33 cm) baking dish as follows:

1. 1 cup (250 mL) meat sauce
2. 4 noodles
3. 1 cup (250 mL) meat sauce
4. Half of mozzarella cheese
5. 1 cup (250 mL) cream sauce
6. 4 noodles
7. 1 cup (250 mL) meat sauce
8. Remaining mozzarella cheese
9. 1 cup (250 mL) cream sauce
10. 4 noodles
11. Remaining meat sauce
12. Remaining cream sauce

Sprinkle with Italian cheese blend. Cover with greased foil. Bake in 375°F (190°C) oven for 1 hour. Remove foil. Bake for about 30 minutes until noodles are tender and cheese is golden. Cool completely. Chill. Cut into 12 squares. Wrap portions in plastic wrap. Freeze. Makes 12 squares.

Directions for reheating I Love Ya Lasagna:

Unwrap frozen lasagna portion. Place on microwave-safe plate. Microwave, covered, on medium (50%) for 2 minutes. Microwave on high (100%) for about 4 minutes until heated through.

1 square: 349 Calories; 16.6 g Total Fat (2.3 g Mono, 0.4 g Poly, 8.6 g Sat); 58 mg Cholesterol; 27 g Carbohydrate; 2 g Fibre; 24 g Protein; 843 mg Sodium

Rosemary Parmesan Crostini

The flavour of rosemary combines with the richness of Parmesan for a delicious and crispy crostini. Perfect for dunking in a warm and comforting bowl of soup, these crisp toasts also make a great partner for Macadamia Chickpea Dip, page 138.

All-purpose flour	2 cups	500 mL
Grated Parmesan cheese	3/4 cup	175 mL
Dried rosemary, crushed	1 1/2 tsp.	7 mL
Baking powder	1 tsp.	5 mL
Salt	1/2 tsp.	2 mL
Cold butter (or hard margarine), cut up	3 tbsp.	50 mL
Large eggs	2	2
Milk	1/2 cup	125 mL
Large egg, fork-beaten	1	1
Grated Parmesan cheese	2 tbsp.	30 mL
Dried rosemary, crushed	1/2 tsp.	2 mL

Combine first 5 ingredients in large bowl. Cut in butter until mixture resembles coarse crumbs.

Whisk eggs and milk in medium bowl. Slowly add to flour mixture, stirring constantly until soft dough forms. Turn out onto lightly floured surface. Divide dough in half. Roll each half into 9 inch (22 cm) long log. Place about 3 inches (7.5 cm) apart on ungreased baking sheet. Flatten logs slightly.

Brush logs with egg. Sprinkle with second amounts of cheese and rosemary. Bake in 350°F (175°C) oven for about 30 minutes until golden. Remove from oven. Let stand on baking sheet for about 10 minutes until cool enough to handle. Using serrated knife, cut each log diagonally into 1/4 inch (6 mm) slices. Arrange, cut-side down, on ungreased baking sheets. Reduce heat to 300°F (150°C). Bake for about 40 minutes, turning at halftime, until dry and crisp. Let stand on baking sheets for 5 minutes before removing to wire rack to cool. Makes about 50 crostini.

1 crostini: 36 Calories; 1.6 g Total Fat (0.2 g Mono, trace Poly, 1.0 g Sat); 17 mg Cholesterol; 4 g Carbohydrate; trace Fibre; 2 g Protein; 80 mg Sodium

Pictured above.

Rustic Apple and Apricot Tart

This rustic-looking tart is much easier to put together than a traditional pie, and it's every bit as elegant. Dried apricots add a sweet, floral note to the traditional apple filling. Dust with icing sugar or serve with ice cream or whipped cream to add a touch more sweetness.

Dried apricots, halved	10	10
Boiling water	1 cup	250 mL
All-purpose flour	1 1/2 cups	375 mL
Cold butter (or hard margarine), cut up	1/2 cup	125 mL
Salt	1/2 tsp.	2 mL
Ice water	3 tbsp.	50 mL
Butter (or hard margarine)	1 tbsp.	15 mL
Medium peeled tart apples (such as Granny Smith), cut into 1/2 inch (12 mm) slices	5	5
Granulated sugar	3 tbsp.	50 mL
Ground cinnamon	1/4 tsp.	1 mL
Granulated sugar	1 tbsp.	15 mL

Put apricot into small heatproof bowl. Add boiling water. Stir. Let stand for about 20 minutes until cool. Drain. Set aside.

Process next 3 ingredients in food processor until mixture resembles coarse crumbs. Add water. Process with on/off motion until mixture starts to come together. Do not over process. Turn out onto lightly floured surface. Shape pastry into disc. Wrap with plastic wrap. Chill for 30 minutes.

Melt second amount of butter in large frying pan on medium. Add next 3 ingredients. Cook for about 12 minutes, stirring occasionally, until apple starts to soften. Add apricot. Stir. Remove from heat. Cool. Roll out pastry on lightly floured surface to 12 inch (30 cm) diameter circle. Transfer to greased baking sheet. Spoon apple mixture onto centre of pastry, leaving 3 inch (7.5 cm) border. Fold section of edge up and over edge of filling. Repeat with next section, allowing pastry to overlap so that fold is created. Repeat until pastry border is completely folded around filling.

Sprinkle second amount of sugar over tart. Bake on bottom rack in 375°F (190°C) oven for 20 minutes. Reduce heat to 350°F (175°C). Bake for about 40 minutes until crust is golden. Let stand on baking sheet until cool. Cuts into 8 wedges.

1 wedge: 280 Calories; 12.9 g Total Fat (3.3 g Mono, 0.5 g Poly, 8.1 g Sat); 34 mg Cholesterol; 40 g Carbohydrate; 3 g Fibre; 3 g Protein; 238 mg Sodium

Pictured at right.

Turkey Chili

Give the new parents a break—and a hearty meal that they're sure to appreciate. Send a jar of this mildly spiced chili along with Cheddar Bacon Cornbread, page 128, for a complete meal.

Cooking oil	1 tsp.	5 mL
Lean ground turkey thigh	1 lb.	454 g
Hot Italian sausage, casing removed	1/2 lb.	225 g
Chopped onion	1 cup	250 mL
Chili powder	2 tbsp.	30 mL
Garlic cloves, minced (or 1/2 tsp., 2 mL, powder)	2	2
Dried oregano	1 tsp.	5 mL
Salt	1/2 tsp.	2 mL
Pepper	1/2 tsp.	2 mL
Can of diced tomatoes (with juice)	28 oz.	796 mL
Can of white kidney beans, rinsed and drained	19 oz.	540 mL
Can of tomato sauce	7 1/2 oz.	213 mL
Granulated sugar	1/2 tsp.	2 mL

Heat cooking oil in large saucepan on medium-high. Add next 8 ingredients. Scramble-fry for about 5 minutes until sausage and turkey start to brown.

Add remaining 4 ingredients. Stir. Bring to a boil. Reduce heat to medium-low. Simmer, covered, for 30 minutes, stirring occasionally, to blend flavours. Cool. Spoon into sterile jars or plastic containers with tight-fitting lids. Makes about 7 cups (1.75 L).

Pictured at right.

Directions for reheating Turkey Chili:

Empty contents of container into saucepan. Cook, covered, on medium for about 20 minutes, stirring occasionally, until heated through. Serves 6.

1 cup (250 mL): 441 Calories; 9.0 g Total Fat (0.4 g Mono, 0.2 g Poly, 1.2 g Sat); 56 mg Cholesterol; 59 g Carbohydrate; 1 g Fibre; 34 g Protein; 903 mg Sodium

---

Top: Turkey Chili, above
Bottom: Rustic Apple and Apricot Tart, this page

Cheddar Bacon Cornbread

The savoury flavours in this hearty cornbread are perfectly balanced with a hint of sweetness from corn. These two yummy loaves are comfort food at its best, and make a delicious addition to any breakfast, lunch, or dinner.

Large eggs, fork-beaten	2	2
Buttermilk (or soured milk, see Tip, below)	1 1/2 cups	375 mL
Yellow cornmeal	1 1/4 cups	300 mL
All-purpose flour	3/4 cup	175 mL
Granulated sugar	1 tbsp.	15 mL
Baking powder	2 tsp.	10 mL
Baking soda	1 tsp.	5 mL
Salt	1/2 tsp.	2 mL
Grated sharp Cheddar cheese	1 1/2 cups	375 mL
Canned (or frozen, thawed) kernel corn	1 cup	250 mL
Thinly sliced green onion	1/2 cup	125 mL
Bacon slices, cooked crisp and crumbled	6	6

Combine first 3 ingredients in medium bowl. Let stand for 15 minutes.

Combine next 5 ingredients in large bowl. Make a well in centre.

Add remaining 4 ingredients and cornmeal mixture to well. Stir until just moistened. Spread evenly in two 5 x 8 inch (12.5 x 20 cm) greased foil loaf pans (see Note). Bake in 375°F (190°C) oven for about 30 minutes until wooden pick inserted in centre of bread comes out clean. Let stand in pan on wire rack until cool. Makes 2 loaves. Each loaf cuts into 8 slices, for a total of 16 slices.

1 slice: 149 Calories; 5.7 g Total Fat (1.6 g Mono, 0.3 g Poly, 3.1 g Sat); 42 mg Cholesterol; 18 g Carbohydrate; 1 g Fibre; 7 g Protein; 618 mg Sodium

Pictured on page 122 and at right.

Note: This size of foil pan comes with a lid that can be used when gifting.

Tip: To make soured milk, measure 1 tbsp. (15 mL) white vinegar or lemon juice into a 1 cup (250 mL) liquid measure. Add enough milk to make 1 cup (250 mL). Stir. Let stand for 1 minute.

Italian Chicken Tomato Sauce

It's hard to beat the classic Italian flavours in this handy dish of chicken sausage in a deliciously rich tomato sauce. Perfect with pasta and garlic toast.

Cooking oil	2 tsp.	10 mL
Chicken (or turkey) sausage, casing removed	13 oz.	370 g
Chopped onion	3/4 cup	175 mL
Dried basil	2 tsp.	10 mL
Dried oregano	1 tsp.	5 mL
Garlic clove, minced (or 1/4 tsp., 1 mL, powder)	1	1
Can of diced tomatoes (with juice)	28 oz.	796 mL
Can of tomato sauce	7 1/2 oz.	213 mL
Granulated sugar	1 tsp.	5 mL

Heat cooking oil in large frying pan on medium-high. Add next 5 ingredients. Scramble-fry for about 10 minutes until sausage is no longer pink.

Add remaining 3 ingredients. Bring to a boil. Reduce heat to medium-low. Simmer, uncovered, for 20 minutes, stirring occasionally, to blend flavours. Cool. Spoon into sterile jars or plastic containers with tight-fitting lids. Makes about 4 3/4 cups (1.2 L).

Pictured at right.

Directions for reheating Italian Chicken Tomato Sauce:

Empty contents of jar into saucepan. Cook, covered, on medium, stirring occasionally, for about 20 minutes until heated through. Serves 4.

3/4 cup (175 mL): 162 Calories; 10.2 g Total Fat (0.8 g Mono, 0.4 g Poly, 2.9 g Sat); 55 mg Cholesterol; 10 g Carbohydrate; 1 g Fibre; 8 g Protein; 973 mg Sodium

---

Left: Cheddar Bacon Cornbread, this page
Right: Italian Chicken Tomato Sauce, above

Mango Lime Trifle

If things seem a bit troubling for someone near and dear to your heart, this sweet treat is just what's needed to make things seem a little bit brighter.

Granulated sugar	1/2 cup	125 mL
Lime juice	1/4 cup	60 mL
Butter (or hard margarine)	2 tbsp.	30 mL
Large eggs, fork-beaten	2	2
Grated lime zest	1 tsp.	5 mL
Whipping cream	1/2 cup	125 mL
Frozen mango pieces, thawed	2 cups	500 mL
Medium sweetened coconut	1/2 cup	125 mL
Mango nectar	1/4 cup	60 mL
Cubed angel food cake	2 cups	500 mL

Lime peel curls, for garnish

Whisk first 3 ingredients in small saucepan on medium for about 3 minutes until sugar is dissolved and butter is melted. Remove from heat.

Whisk eggs in medium bowl until frothy. Gradually whisk lime mixture into eggs. Return mixture to saucepan. Heat and stir on medium for about 3 minutes until mixture is thick enough to coat back of spoon. Do not boil.

Add lime zest. Stir. Transfer to medium bowl. Cover with plastic wrap directly on surface to prevent skin from forming. Chill for about 1 hour until completely cool.

Beat whipping cream in small bowl until stiff peaks form. Fold 1/2 cup (125 mL) whipped cream into lime mixture until no white streaks remain. Reserve remaining whipped cream in bowl.

Combine next 3 ingredients in small bowl.

To assemble, layer ingredients in 1 quart (1 L) glass bowl as follows:

1. Half of cake cubes
2. Half of mango mixture
3. Half of lime mixture
4. Remaining cake cubes
5. Remaining mango mixture
6. Remaining lime curd

Spread or pipe reserved whipped cream in decorative pattern over lime curd.

Garnish with lime peel. Makes about 4 cups (1 L).

1/2 cup (125 mL): 270 Calories; 11.3 g Total Fat (2.5 g Mono, 0.5 g Poly, 7.0 g Sat); 82 mg Cholesterol; 40 g Carbohydrate; 1 g Fibre; 4 g Protein; 268 mg Sodium

Pictured at right.

Turkey Salsa Meatloaves

Meatloaf is the kind of comfort food that people crave when things seem difficult. Bring back happy childhood memories with these tasty and convenient little meatloaves. Ground turkey and salsa add a unique twist to this updated classic.

Large egg, fork-beaten	1	1
Fine dry bread crumbs	2/3 cup	150 mL
Medium salsa	1/3 cup	75 mL
Salt	1 tsp.	5 mL
Pepper	1/2 tsp.	2 mL
Lean ground turkey thigh	1 1/2 lbs.	680 g
Medium salsa	1/4 cup	60 mL
Grated jalapeño Monterey Jack cheese	1/2 cup	125 mL

Combine first 5 ingredients in large bowl. Add turkey. Mix well. Press evenly into 2 greased 5 x 3 x 2 inch (12.5 x 7.5 x 5 cm) loaf pans. Place on baking sheet. Bake in 350°F (175°C) oven for about 50 minutes until internal temperature reaches 175°F (80°C).

Spread second amount of salsa on meatloaves. Sprinkle with cheese. Bake for another 5 minutes until cheese is melted. Let stand until cool. Store in refrigerator for up to 3 days. Makes 2 meatloaves. Each loaf cuts into 10 slices, for a total of 20 slices

Pictured at right.

Directions for reheating Turkey Salsa Meatloaf:

Bake, covered, in 350°F (175°C) oven for about 40 minutes until heated through. Cuts into 10 slices.

1 slice: 151 Calories; 6.9 g Total Fat (0 g Mono, 0 g Poly, 2.4 g Sat); 66 mg Cholesterol; 7 g Carbohydrate; trace Fibre; 16 g Protein; 488 mg Sodium

---

Top: Turkey Salsa Meatloaves, above
Bottom: Mango Lime Trifle, this page

Bacon Herb Quiche

A simple and delicious recipe becomes thoughtful and kind when you prepare it and give it to someone who has recently moved into a new home.

Pastry for 9 inch (22 cm) pie shell		
Bacon slices	6	6
Chopped fresh white mushrooms	1 cup	250 mL
Chopped onion	1 cup	250 mL
Grated sharp Cheddar cheese	1/2 cup	125 mL
Chopped fresh basil	1/4 cup	60 mL
Large eggs	4	4
Milk	1 cup	250 mL
Salt	1/8 tsp.	0.5 mL
Pepper	1/8 tsp.	0.5 mL

Roll out pastry on lightly floured surface to 1/8 inch (3 mm) thickness. Line 9 inch (22 cm) deep dish foil pie plate. Trim, leaving 1/2 inch (12 mm) overhang. Roll under and crimp decorative edge.

Cook bacon in large frying pan on medium until crisp. Remove to paper towel-lined plate to drain. Crumble. Set aside.

Drain and discard all but 1 tsp. (5 mL) drippings. Add mushrooms and onion to same frying pan. Cook for about 10 minutes, stirring occasionally, until onion is softened and starting to brown. Let stand for 5 minutes to cool slightly. Spoon into pie shell.

Scatter cheese, basil and bacon over onion mixture.

Whisk next 4 ingredients in medium bowl. Pour over cheese mixture. Bake on bottom rack in 375°F (190°C) oven for about 45 minutes until knife inserted in centre of quiche comes out clean. Cool. Store, covered, in refrigerator for up to 3 days. Cuts into 6 wedges.

Pictured at right.

Directions for reheating Bacon Herb Quiche:

Cover with foil. Bake in 400°F (205°C) oven for about 20 minutes until heated through. Serves 6.

1 wedge: 318 Calories; 19.3 g Total Fat (2.6 g Mono, 0.5 g Poly, 8.4 g Sat); 170 mg Cholesterol; 24 g Carbohydrate; trace Fibre; 12 g Protein; 454 mg Sodium

---

Super Spinach Salad Kit

It can often be difficult to eat right when you're going through stressful times. Make-your-own salad kits ensure proper nutrition, as well as being a unique and thoughtful gift! Package each component separately so the salad can be tossed together for a quick bite.

CREAMY DRESSING		
Cooking oil	3 tbsp.	50 mL
Mayonnaise	3 tbsp.	50 mL
White vinegar	3 tbsp.	50 mL
Granulated sugar	2 tbsp.	30 mL
Garlic powder	1/8 tsp.	0.5 mL
Onion powder	1/8 tsp.	0.5 mL
Salt	1/8 tsp.	0.5 mL
SALAD KIT		
Dark raisins	3 tbsp.	50 mL
Dried cranberries	3 tbsp.	50 mL
Chopped pecans, toasted (see Tip, page 41)	1/4 cup	60 mL
Salted, roasted sunflower seeds	1/4 cup	60 mL
Bag of fresh spinach	6 oz.	170 g

Creamy Dressing: Whisk all 7 ingredients in small bowl until smooth. Pour into jar with tight-fitting lid. Makes about 2/3 cup (150 mL).

Salad Kit: Combine raisins and cranberries in small resealable freezer bag.

Combine pecans and sunflower seeds in separate small resealable freezer bag.

Put bag of spinach into large resealable freezer bag. Add jar of dressing, bag of fruit mixture and bag of nut mixture. Seal bag. Keep refrigerated.

Pictured at right.

Directions for Super Spinach Salad:

Put spinach into large bowl. Add contents of freezer bags. Drizzle with 1/3 cup (75 mL) dressing. Toss until coated. Store leftover dressing in refrigerator for up to 3 weeks. Makes about 6 1/2 cups (1.6 L).

1 cup (250 mL) salad: 160 Calories; 12.2 g Total Fat (3.7 g Mono, 2.0 g Poly, 1.3 g Sat); 1 mg Cholesterol; 11 g Carbohydrate; 2 g Fibre; 3 g Protein; 82 mg Sodium

---

Top: Super Spinach Salad Kit, above
Bottom: Bacon Herb Quiche, this page

Restore Your Energy Bars

When someone's feeling a little under the weather, a quick burst of energy can help a lot. Once these bars are completely cooled, cut and wrap them individually for a quick snack while on the path to recovery.

Pitted dates	2 cups	500 mL
Carrot juice	1 cup	250 mL
Chopped dried apricot	1 cup	250 mL
Butter (or hard margarine), softened	1 cup	250 mL
Brown sugar, packed	1 cup	250 mL
Whole-wheat flour	2 cups	500 mL
Large flake rolled oats	1 cup	250 mL
Bran flakes cereal	3/4 cup	175 mL
Ground cinnamon	1 tsp.	5 mL

Line 9 x 13 inch (22 x 33 cm) pan with greased foil, leaving 2 inch (5 cm) overhang on 2 sides. Combine first 3 ingredients in medium saucepan. Bring to a boil. Reduce heat to medium-low. Simmer, covered, for about 12 minutes, stirring occasionally, until apricot is soft and liquid is absorbed. Let stand for 10 minutes. Beat for about 2 minutes until smooth. Set aside.

Beat butter and brown sugar with same beaters in large bowl until light and fluffy.

Add flour. Beat until smooth. Add remaining 3 ingredients. Stir. Press 2 cups (500 mL) oat mixture firmly in prepared pan. Spread date mixture evenly over bottom layer. Sprinkle with remaining oat mixture. Press down gently. Bake in 375°F (190°C) oven for about 25 minutes until lightly browned. Let stand in pan on wire rack until cool. Holding edges of foil, remove bars from pan. Cut into 1 x 2 1/2 inch (2.5 x 6.4 cm) bars. Wrap with plastic wrap. Makes about 33 bars.

1 bar: 153 Calories; 5.8 g Total Fat (1.4 g Mono, 0.3 g Poly, 3.5 g Sat); 15 mg Cholesterol; 25 g Carbohydrate; 2 g Fibre; 2 g Protein; 56 mg Sodium

Pictured at right.

Banana Cranberry Oat Loaf

Craft stores often carry attractively decorated, seasonally inspired ceramic loaf pans that are quite inexpensive. Bake these loaves in ceramic pans and half of your gift-wrapping is already done!

All-purpose flour	2 cups	500 mL
Brown sugar, packed	1 cup	250 mL
Quick-cooking rolled oats	1 cup	250 mL
Baking powder	2 tsp.	10 mL
Baking soda	1 tsp.	5 mL
Ground cinnamon	1/2 tsp.	2 mL
Salt	1/2 tsp.	2 mL
Large egg	1	1
Mashed overripe banana (about 3 small)	1 cup	250 mL
Buttermilk (or soured milk, see Tip, page 128)	1/2 cup	125 mL
Cooking oil	1/3 cup	75 mL
Vanilla extract	1 tsp.	5 mL
Frozen (or fresh) cranberries, thawed, chopped	1 1/2 cups	375 mL

Combine first 7 ingredients in large bowl. Make a well in centre.

Beat next 5 ingredients in medium bowl until smooth.

Add cranberries. Stir. Add to well. Stir until just moistened. Spread evenly in 4 greased 3 x 5 inch (7.5 x 12.5 cm) foil loaf pans. Bake in 350°F (175°C) oven for about 35 minutes until wooden pick inserted in centre of loaf comes out clean. Let stand in pan for 10 minutes before removing to wire rack to cool. Makes 4 loaves. Each loaf cuts into 8 slices, for a total of 32 slices.

1 slice: 98 Calories; 2.8 g Total Fat (1.4 g Mono, 0.7 g Poly, 0.3 g Sat); 7 mg Cholesterol; 17 g Carbohydrate; 1 g Fibre; 2 g Protein; 118 mg Sodium

Pictured at right.

Top: Restore Your Energy Bars, this page
Bottom: Banana Cranberry Oat Loaf, above

Chai Bread Ring

Bread with the soothing comfort of chai tea flavours and an attractive presentation. This gift isn't only thoughtful, it's impressive!

Warm water	1/4 cup	60 mL
Granulated sugar	1 tsp.	5 mL
Envelope of active dry yeast (or 2 1/4 tsp.,11 mL)	1/4 oz.	8 g
Large eggs, room temperature	3	3
All-purpose flour	1 cup	250 mL
Warm milk (see Note)	3/4 cup	175 mL
Butter, melted	1/2 cup	125 mL
Salt	1 tsp.	5 mL
Vanilla extract	1 tsp.	5 mL
All-purpose flour	3 cups	750 mL
All-purpose flour, approximately	1/3 cup	75 mL
Butter, melted	1/4 cup	60 mL
Brown sugar, packed	1/2 cup	125 mL
Ground ginger	1 tbsp.	15 mL
Ground cardamom	1 tsp.	5 mL
Ground cinnamon	1 tsp.	5 mL
Ground nutmeg	1/2 tsp.	2 mL
Coarsely ground pepper	1/4 tsp.	1 mL
Ground cloves	1/4 tsp.	1 mL
Butter, melted	1 1/2 tsp.	7 mL

Stir warm water and sugar in small bowl until sugar is dissolved. Sprinkle yeast over top. Let stand for 10 minutes. Stir until yeast is dissolved.

Whisk next 6 ingredients in large bowl. Add yeast mixture. Whisk until smooth.

Add second amount of flour, 1/2 cup (125 mL) at a time, stirring well after each addition, until soft dough forms. Turn out onto lightly floured surface.

Knead for about 5 minutes until smooth, adding third amount of flour 1 tbsp. (15 mL) at a time, if necessary, to prevent sticking. Dough should still be soft. Place in greased extra-large bowl, turning once to grease top. Cover with greased waxed paper and tea towel. Let stand in oven with light on and door closed for about 1 hour until doubled in bulk. Punch dough down. Turn out onto lightly floured surface. Knead for about 1 minute until smooth. Roll out dough to 12 x 16 inch (30 x 40 cm) rectangle.

Brush with second amount of melted butter. Combine next 7 ingredients in small bowl. Sprinkle over dough, leaving 1/2 inch (12 mm) edge on all sides. Roll up from long edge, jelly-roll style. Pinch seam to seal. Holding 1 end of roll, twist dough about 5 or 6 times. Place in greased 10 inch (25 cm) tube pan. Pinch ends together. Cover with greased waxed paper and tea towel. Let stand in oven with light on and door closed for about 1 hour until doubled in bulk. Bake in 350°F (175°C) oven for about 45 minutes until golden and hollow-sounding when tapped. Let stand in pan for 5 minutes.

Brush with third amount of melted butter. Remove bread from pan and place on wire rack to cool. Cuts into 16 slices.

1 slice: 232 Calories; 9.7 g Total Fat (2.4 g Mono, 0.4 g Poly, 5.9 g Sat); 51 mg Cholesterol; 32 g Carbohydrate; 1 g Fibre; 5 g Protein; 228 mg Sodium

Pictured below.

Note: Milk can be heated in the microwave on medium (50%) for about 1 minute.

Potato Parmesan Braids

For that person who's worth a little extra effort—the braiding takes some time, but the result is a stunning loaf that anyone would be thrilled to receive.

Chopped peeled potato	2 cups	500 mL
Butter (or hard margarine)	6 tbsp.	100 mL
Granulated sugar	1 tbsp.	15 mL
Salt	1 1/2 tsp.	7 mL
Whole-wheat flour	2 1/2 cups	625 mL
Grated Parmesan cheese	1 cup	250 mL
Envelope of instant yeast (or 2 1/4 tsp., 11 mL)	1/4 oz.	8 g
All-purpose flour	3 1/2 cups	875 mL
All-purpose flour, approximately	1/4 cup	60 mL
Butter (or hard margarine), melted	2 tsp.	10 mL

Pour water into medium saucepan until about 1 inch (2.5 cm) deep. Add potato. Cover. Bring to a boil. Reduce heat to medium. Boil gently, uncovered, for 12 to 15 minutes until tender. Drain, reserving 2 cups (500 mL) potato water in small bowl. Return potatoes to same pot. Mash.

Add potato water and next 3 ingredients. Stir until butter is melted. Transfer to large bowl. Let stand for about 10 minutes until lukewarm.

Add next 3 ingredients. Beat with spoon for 2 minutes.

Add first amount of all-purpose flour. Mix until soft dough forms.

Turn out onto lightly floured surface. Knead for 5 to 8 minutes until smooth and elastic, adding second amount of all-purpose flour 1 tbsp. (15 mL) at a time, if necessary, to prevent sticking. Place in greased extra-large bowl, turning once to grease top. Cover with greased waxed paper and tea towel. Let stand in oven with light on and door closed for about 45 minutes until doubled in bulk. Punch dough down. Divide dough in half. Divide first half into 3 equal portions. Roll out each portion on lightly floured surface to 12 inch (30 cm) long rope with slightly tapered ends. Lay ropes, side-by-side, on greased baking sheet. Pinch ropes together at 1 end. Braid ropes. Pinch together at opposite end. Tuck ends under. Repeat with second half of dough on same baking sheet. Cover with greased waxed paper and tea towel. Let stand in oven with light on and door closed for about 30 minutes until almost doubled in size. Bake in 350°F (175°C) oven for about 35 minutes until golden and hollow sounding when tapped.

Brush hot loaves with melted butter. Remove from baking sheet and place on wire rack to cool. Makes 2 loaves. Each loaf cuts into 20 slices, for a total of 40 slices.

1 slice: 100 Calories; 3.0 g Total Fat (0.5 g Mono, 0.1 g Poly, 1.8 g Sat); 8 mg Cholesterol; 16 g Carbohydrate; 1 g Fibre; 4 g Protein; 153 mg Sodium

Pictured below.

Macadamia Chickpea Dip

*This family-friendly dip can be stored in the refrigerator
for up to three weeks and goes great with
Rosemary Parmesan Crostini, page 125.*

Can of chickpeas (garbanzo beans), rinsed and drained	19 oz.	540 mL
Salted, roasted macadamia nuts	1/2 cup	125 mL
Olive (or cooking) oil	3 tbsp.	50 mL
Chopped fresh basil	2 tbsp.	30 mL
Orange juice	2 tbsp.	30 mL
Lime juice	1 tbsp.	15 mL
Garlic clove, minced (or 1/4 tsp., 1 mL, powder)	1	1
Salt, just a pinch		
Pepper, just a pinch		

Process all 9 ingredients in food processor until smooth. Spoon
into jar with tight-fitting lid. Makes about 2 1/2 cups (625 mL).

*1/4 cup (60 mL): 127 Calories; 9.8 g Total Fat (6.9 g Mono, 1.1 g Poly, 1.4 g Sat);
0 mg Cholesterol; 9 g Carbohydrate; 3 g Fibre; 3 g Protein; 73 mg Sodium*

Dilled Orzo and Rice Mix

*This dry mix is just the solution for the friend who's really
in a pickle. Sure to please the entire family.*

Orzo	2/3 cup	150 mL
Long grain white rice	1/2 cup	125 mL
Dried dillweed	2 tsp.	10 mL
Dried basil	1/4 tsp.	1 mL
Garlic powder	1/4 tsp.	1 mL
Salt	1/4 tsp.	1 mL
Pepper	1/4 tsp.	1 mL

Combine all 7 ingredients in small bowl. Spoon into jar with
tight-fitting lid. Makes about 1 1/4 cups (300 mL).

Pictured at right.

Directions for Dilled Orzo and Rice:

Heat 1 tsp. (5 mL) cooking oil in medium saucepan on
medium. Add 1 cup (250 mL) chopped onion. Cook for
about 7 minutes, stirring often, until onion starts to brown.
Add contents of jar. Heat and stir for 1 minute. Add 2 3/4 cups
(675 mL) prepared chicken broth. Bring to a boil. Reduce
heat to medium-low. Simmer, covered, for about 20 minutes,
without stirring, until orzo and rice are tender and liquid
is absorbed. Remove from heat. Let stand, covered, for
5 minutes. Fluff with fork. Makes about 3 2/3 cups (900 mL).

*1/2 cup (125 mL) pilaf: 122 Calories; 1.0 g Total Fat (0.4 g Mono, 0.2 g Poly, 0.1 g
Sat); 0 mg Cholesterol; 25 g Carbohydrate; 1 g Fibre; 3 g Protein; 237 mg Sodium*

Jewelled Barley Pilaf Mix

*This dry mix is a great combination of nutritious barley,
delicious Moroccan spices and sweet dried fruit.
With just a few minutes of work, the lucky recipient
will have a winning side dish.*

Pearl barley	1 cup	250 mL
Chopped dried apricot	3 tbsp.	50 mL
Dried cranberries	3 tbsp.	50 mL
Golden raisins	2 tbsp.	30 mL
Ground cinnamon	1 tsp.	5 mL
Turmeric	1/2 tsp.	2 mL
Ground cardamom	1/4 tsp.	1 mL
Ground nutmeg	1/4 tsp.	1 mL
Salt	1/2 tsp.	2 mL
Pepper	1/4 tsp.	1 mL

Combine all 10 ingredients in small bowl. Spoon into jar
with tight-fitting lid. Makes about 1 1/2 cups (375 mL).

Pictured at right.

Directions for Jewelled Barley Pilaf:

Heat 2 tbsp. (30 mL) butter (or hard margarine) in large
saucepan on medium. Add contents of jar. Heat and stir for
about 2 minutes until barley is coated. Add 3 cups (750 mL)
water. Bring to a boil. Reduce heat to medium-low. Simmer,
covered, for about 30 minutes, without stirring. Remove from
heat. Let stand, covered, for about 10 minutes until liquid
is absorbed and barley is tender. Fluff with fork. Makes about
3 1/2 cups (875 mL).

*1/2 cup (125 mL) pilaf: 162 Calories; 3.9 g Total Fat (0.9 g Mono, 0.1 g Poly,
2.1 g Sat); 9 mg Cholesterol; 30 g Carbohydrate; 5 g Fibre; 3 g Protein;
195 mg Sodium*

Clockwise from Left:
Burger Booster Mix, below
Jewelled Barley Pilaf Mix, left
Dilled Orzo And Rice Mix, left

Burger Booster Mix

For those that haven't yet figured out their way around the kitchen, this handy pasta dish takes little effort and only requires the addition of hamburger. Now aren't you helpful!

Envelope of tomato basil soup mix	2.9 oz.	82 g
Thinly sliced sun-dried tomatoes	1/4 cup	60 mL
Packets of beef bouillon powder (1 tbsp., 15 mL)	2	2
Italian seasoning	1 tbsp.	15 mL
Minced onion flakes	1 tbsp.	15 mL
Dried crushed chilies	1/2 tsp.	2 mL
Pepper	1/2 tsp.	2 mL
Garlic powder	1/4 tsp.	1 mL
Rotini pasta	2 cups	500 mL

Combine first 8 ingredients in small bowl. Spoon into jar with tight-fitting lid.

Add pasta to jar. Makes about 3 cups (750 mL).

Pictured above.

Directions for Burger Booster:

Heat 1 tsp. (5 mL) cooking oil in Dutch oven on medium-high. Scramble-fry 1 1/2 lbs. (680 g) lean ground beef until browned. Add 5 cups (1.25 L) water and contents of jar. Stir. Bring to a boil, stirring occasionally. Reduce heat to medium-low. Simmer, covered, for about 20 minutes, stirring often, until pasta is tender but firm. Remove from heat. Let stand, covered, for about 10 minutes until any remaining liquid is absorbed. Makes about 7 cups (1.75 L).

1 1/2 cups (375 mL): 466 Calories; 17.7 g Total Fat (0.7 g Mono, 0.3 g Poly, 6.6 g Sat); 96 mg Cholesterol; 39 g Carbohydrate; 3 g Fibre; 36 g Protein; 966 mg Sodium

---

Hearty Beef Stew

Nothing says comfort like a bowl of hot stew.
For a truly hearty dinner, you can bulk this meal
up with some biscuits or bread.

Cooking oil	1 1/2 tbsp.	25 mL
Boneless beef blade steak, cut into 1 inch (2.5 cm) pieces	2 lbs.	900 g
Prepared beef broth	2 cups	500 mL
Can of diced tomatoes (with juice)	14 oz.	398 mL
Chopped onion	1 1/2 cups	375 mL
Garlic cloves, minced (or 1/2 tsp., 2 mL, powder)	2	2
Dried thyme	1 tsp.	5 mL
Bay leaf	1	1
Salt	1/2 tsp.	2 mL
Diced carrot	2 cups	500 mL
Cubed yellow turnip	1 cup	250 mL
Chopped celery	1/2 cup	125 mL
Water	2 tbsp.	30 mL
All-purpose flour	2 tbsp.	30 mL

Heat cooking oil in large frying pan on medium-high. Add beef. Cook for about 10 minutes, stirring occasionally, until browned. Transfer to ungreased 3 quart (3 L) casserole.

Add next 7 ingredients to same frying pan. Bring to a boil, stirring constantly and scraping any brown bits from bottom of pan. Add to beef. Stir. Cook, covered, in 325°F (160°C) oven for 1 1/2 hours.

Add next 3 ingredients. Stir. Cook, covered, for about 45 minutes until vegetables are almost tender.

Stir water into flour in small cup until smooth. Slowly add to beef mixture, stirring constantly, until combined. Cook, uncovered, for about 30 minutes, stirring once, until boiling and thickened. Cool. Store, covered, in refrigerator for up to 3 days. Makes about 5 1/2 cups (1.4 L).

Pictured at right.

Directions for reheating Hearty Beef Stew:

Place stew in 2 quart (2L) casserole dish. Bake, covered, in 325°F (160°C) oven for about 30 minutes until heated through.

1 cup (250 mL): 399 Calories; 21.6 g Total Fat (9.1 g Mono, 2.0 g Poly, 6.9 g Sat); 109 mg Cholesterol; 17 g Carbohydrate; 3 g Fibre; 34 g Protein; 1084 mg Sodium

---

Fruity Snack Cake

This cake is packed with all the nutritious stuff you
need and plenty of sweetness, too. Treats like these
are just what people need to brighten their days.

Whole-wheat flour	2 cups	500 mL
All-purpose flour	1 cup	250 mL
Baking powder	2 tsp.	10 mL
Baking soda	1 tsp.	5 mL
Ground cinnamon	1 tsp.	5 mL
Salt	1/2 tsp.	2 mL
Large eggs	2	2
Applesauce	1 cup	250 mL
Brown sugar, packed	1 cup	250 mL
Vanilla yogurt	1 cup	250 mL
Cooking oil	1/3 cup	75 mL
Golden raisins	1 1/2 cups	375 mL
Raw pumpkin seeds, toasted (see Tip, page 41)	1/2 cup	125 mL
Raw sunflower seeds, toasted (see Tip, page 41)	1/2 cup	125 mL

Line 9 x 13 inch (22 x 33 cm) pan with greased foil, leaving a 2 inch (5 cm) overhang on 2 sides. Set aside. Combine first 6 ingredients in large bowl. Make a well in centre.

Whisk next 5 ingredients in medium bowl until smooth. Add remaining 3 ingredients. Stir. Add to well. Stir until just moistened. Spread evenly in prepared pan. Bake in 350°F (175°C) oven for about 35 minutes until wooden pick inserted in centre of cake comes out clean. Let stand in pan until cool. Holding foil, remove cake from pan. Cut into 1 x 4 inch (2.5 x 10 cm) bars. Wrap with plastic wrap. Makes about 24 bars.

1 bar: 206 Calories; 7.3 g Total Fat (1.8 g Mono, 1.0 g Poly, 0.9 g Sat); 19 mg Cholesterol; 32 g Carbohydrate; 2 g Fibre; 5 g Protein; 172 mg Sodium

Pictured at right.

Top: Fruity Snack Cake, above
Bottom: Hearty Beef Stew, this page

Breakfast Malt Bread

This mild malt-flavoured bread is simply great toasted, and even better when it's topped with butter, honey or marmalade. The perfect solution to the breakfast conundrum.

Envelope of instant yeast (or 2 1/4 tsp., 11 mL)	1/4 oz.	8 g
Whole-wheat flour	2 cups	500 mL
Water	1 1/3 cups	325 mL
Ovaltine	1/2 cup	125 mL
Cooking oil	3 tbsp.	50 mL
Fancy (mild) molasses	2 tbsp.	30 mL
Brown sugar, packed	1 1/2 tbsp.	25 mL
Salt	2 tsp.	10 mL
All-purpose flour	2 cups	500 mL
All-purpose flour, approximately	1 tbsp.	15 mL

Combine yeast and whole-wheat flour in small bowl.

Combine next 6 ingredients in medium saucepan. Heat and stir on medium for about 5 minutes until very warm. Transfer to large bowl. Add yeast mixture. Whisk until soft, sticky dough forms.

Add first amount of all-purpose flour, 1/2 cup (125 mL) at a time, stirring well after each addition, until stiff dough forms.

Turn out onto lightly floured surface. Knead for 8 to 10 minutes until smooth and elastic, adding second amount of all-purpose flour, if necessary, to prevent sticking. Place in greased extra-large bowl, turning once to grease top. Cover with greased waxed paper and tea towel. Let stand in oven with light on and door closed for about 1 hour until doubled in bulk. Punch dough down. Knead 6 times. Divide dough into 2 equal portions. Shape portions into 12 inch (30 cm) long loaves. Place loaves diagonally, about 3 inches (7.5 cm) apart, on greased baking sheet. Cover with greased waxed paper and tea towel. Let stand in oven with light on and door closed for about 50 minutes until doubled in size. Using sharp knife, cut 3 slashes diagonally across top of each loaf. Bake in 350°F (175°C) oven for about 30 minutes until golden brown and hollow-sounding when tapped. Remove loaves from baking sheet and place on wire racks to cool. Makes 2 loaves. Each loaf cuts into 20 slices, for a total of 40 slices.

1 slice: 59 Calories; 1.2 g Total Fat (0.6 g Mono, 0.4 g Poly, 0.1 g Sat); 0 mg Cholesterol; 11 g Carbohydrate; 1 g Fibre; 2 g Protein; 123 mg Sodium

Pictured at right.

Whole-Wheat Lemon Herb Bread

Rosemary and lemon are like best friends in this fantastic whole-wheat loaf.

Warm water	1/2 cup	125 mL
Granulated sugar	1 tsp.	5 mL
Envelope of active dry yeast (or 2 1/4 tsp.,11 mL)	1/4 oz.	8 g
Warm buttermilk	1 cup	250 mL
Warm water	1 cup	250 mL
Cooking oil	1/4 cup	60 mL
Liquid honey	1/4 cup	60 mL
All-purpose flour	3 cups	750 mL
Whole-wheat flour	3 cups	750 mL
Chopped fresh rosemary (or 3/4 tsp., 4 mL, dried, crushed)	1 tbsp.	15 mL
Grated lemon zest	1 tbsp.	15 mL
Salt	1 tbsp.	15 mL
Coarsely ground pepper	2 tsp.	10 mL
All-purpose flour, approximately	2 tbsp.	30 mL
Large egg, fork-beaten	1	1
Water	1 tsp.	5 mL

Stir warm water and sugar in small bowl until sugar is dissolved. Sprinkle yeast over top. Let stand for 10 minutes. Stir until yeast is dissolved.

Whisk next 4 ingredients in medium bowl. Add yeast mixture. Whisk until smooth.

Combine next 6 ingredients in large bowl. Add yeast mixture. Mix until soft dough forms. Turn out onto lightly floured surface.

Knead for about 10 minutes until smooth and elastic, adding second amount of all-purpose flour 1 tbsp. (15 mL) at a time, if necessary, to prevent sticking. Place in greased extra-large bowl, turning once to grease top. Cover with greased waxed paper and tea towel. Let stand in oven with light on and door closed for about 1 hour until doubled in bulk. Punch dough down. Turn out onto lightly floured surface. Knead for about 1 minute until smooth. Divide dough into 2 equal portions. Shape portions into balls. Place on greased large baking sheet. Cover with greased wax paper and tea towel. Let stand in oven with light on and door closed for about 30 minutes until doubled in size.

Whisk egg and water in small cup. Brush over loaves. Bake on centre rack in 350°F (175°C) oven for about 30 minutes until hollow-sounding when tapped. Remove loaves from baking sheet and place on wire rack to cool. Makes 2 loaves. Each loaf cuts into 12 slices, for a total of 24 slices.

1 slice: 145 Calories; 3.0 g Total Fat (1.4 g Mono, 0.8 g Poly, 0.4 g Sat); 10 mg Cholesterol; 26 g Carbohydrate; 2 g Fibre; 4 g Protein; 304 mg Sodium

Pictured at right.

Top: Whole-Wheat Lemon Herb Bread, above
Bottom: Breakfast Malt Bread, this page

Kids Can Craft

Hey kids! This is the section for you—no grown-ups allowed! Of course you have to ask for permission before you start cooking, and maybe you'll need a little help from Mom or Dad if you haven't quite figured out your way around the kitchen yet. All these crafty little kitchen treats and art projects are designed to help you give your parents, friends or teachers a special gift that you've made yourself.

Caramel Candy Apples, page 155

Chocolate Sours, below, with Goodie Catcher, page 146

Chocolate Sours

What could possibly make gummy candies any better?
Chocolate, of course! Impress your friends with these
deliciously sweet-and-sour candies that you made yourself.
Pack them into a Goodie Catcher, page 146, for a super-cool
birthday present for your best buddy.

Chocolate melting wafers	1 cup	250 mL
Sour gummy cherry candies	1/4 cup	60 mL
Sour jujubes	1/4 cup	60 mL
Sour gummy rings	1/4 cup	60 mL
Gummy bears	1/4 cup	60 mL

Put chocolate wafers into small microwave-safe bowl (see Tip, page 12). Microwave, uncovered, on medium (50%), stirring every 30 seconds, until almost melted. Stir until smooth.

Dip remaining 4 ingredients, 1 piece at a time, into chocolate, allowing excess to drip back into bowl (see Tip, page 154). Place on waxed paper-lined baking sheet. Let stand until set. Makes about 64 pieces.

1 piece: 33 Calories; 1.0 g Total Fat (0.0 g Mono, 0.0 g Poly, 0.8 g Sat); 0 mg Cholesterol; 6 g Carbohydrate; trace Fibre; trace Protein; 10 mg Sodium

Pictured above.

Goodie Catcher

This is a traditional origami fold that has been turned into a fun children's game. It also makes a fun holder for little homemade treats, like Chocolate Sours, page 145— perfect for kids to make as a birthday gift for a friend!

MATERIALS
10 inch (25 cm) square of lightweight cardstock

TOOLS
coloured markers

Follow the diagram to make the folds. When you are done, decorate the outside squares with names of colours. Open the inside flaps and write different numbers on each of the 8 triangles. Open the next set of flaps and write a fun fortune on the inside of each.

HOW TO PLAY

Some fun fortune ideas:

You will have many good hair days.

You will be a star in your next game.

Someday you'll be famous.

You will do something kind for someone this week.

You will have a big surprise soon.

You will go somewhere cool this summer.

To play:

1. Put your fingers and thumbs in the 4 gaps on the back side of the goodie catcher.

2. Get your friend to pick a colour from the outside flaps.

3. By moving the game back and forth with your fingers and thumb, spell out the colour.

4. Have your friend pick a number from the inside flaps.

5. Move the game back and forth as you count that number out.

6. Let your friend pick one more number.

7. Open that flap and read their fortune aloud.

Pictured on page 145.

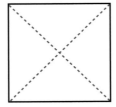

1. Fold, pattern-side up, on both diagonals. Unfold.

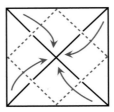

2. Fold all four corners to centre.

3. Turn paper over.

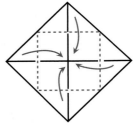

4. Again, fold all four corners to centre.

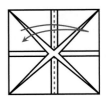

5. Fold paper in half and unfold.

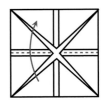

6. Fold in half from top to bottom. Do not unfold.

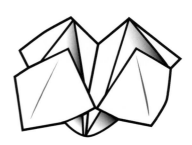

Top: Bread Stick Bones, page 148
Bottom: Seven Seas Snack Mix, page 148

Seven Seas Snack Mix

Barnacles, driftwood, seashells and goldfish—
a snack mix any pirate would treasure!

Cone-shaped corn snacks	1 1/2 cups	375 mL
Goldfish crackers	1 1/2 cups	375 mL
"O"–shaped toasted oat cereal	1 1/2 cups	375 mL
Stick pretzels	1 1/2 cups	375 mL
Instant butterscotch pudding powder (half of 4-serving size)	1/3 cup	75 mL
Ground cinnamon	2 tsp.	10 mL
Chili powder	2 tsp.	10 mL
Butter, melted	1/4 cup	60 mL

Combine first 4 ingredients in medium roasting pan.

Combine next 3 ingredients in small bowl.

Drizzle half of melted butter over pretzel mixture. Toss until coated. Sprinkle with half of spice mixture. Toss well. Repeat with remaining butter and spice mixture. Bake, uncovered, in 300°F (150°C) oven for about 15 minutes, stirring occasionally, until lightly toasted. Makes about 6 cups (1.5 L).

1/2 cup (125 mL): 182 Calories; 7.5 g Total Fat (2.2 g Mono, 0.9 g Poly, 3.8 g Sat); 11 mg Cholesterol; 25 g Carbohydrate; 1 g Fibre; 3 g Protein; 345 mg Sodium

Pictured on page 147.

Bread Stick Bones

You won't need sticks and stones to break these bones—
bite into these delicious bone-shaped breadsticks instead.
They're coated with yummy cinnamon and sugar!

Tube of refrigerated bread sticks	11 oz.	310 g
Butter (or hard margarine), melted	2 tbsp.	30 mL
Granulated sugar	2 tbsp.	30 mL
Ground cinnamon	2 tsp.	10 mL

Cut dough sheet along perforated lines. Tie ends of dough strips into loose knots. Arrange about 1 inch (2.5 cm) apart on greased baking sheet.

Brush with melted butter.

Combine sugar and cinnamon in small cup. Sprinkle over dough. Bake in 375°F (190°C) oven for about 12 minutes until browned. Let stand on baking sheet for 5 minutes before removing to wire rack to cool. Makes 8 bread sticks.

1 bread stick: 149 Calories; 4.9 g Total Fat (0.7 g Mono, 0.1 g Poly, 1.8 g Sat); 7.5 mg Cholesterol; 23 g Carbohydrate; 1 g Fibre; 3 g Protein; 310 mg Sodium

Pictured on page 147.

Vanilla Fruit Salad

Show mom how much you care with a
bowl of this refreshing fruit salad! Perfect for
a Mother's Day breakfast in bed.

Vanilla yogurt	1 cup	250 mL
Ground cinnamon	1/4 tsp.	1 mL
Can of pineapple chunks, drained	14 oz.	398 mL
Can of mandarin orange segments, drained	10 oz.	284 mL
Fresh (or frozen, thawed) strawberries, quartered	1 cup	250 mL
Sliced banana (1/2 inch, 12 mm, slices)	3/4 cup	175 mL

Combine yogurt and cinnamon in medium bowl.

Add remaining 4 ingredients. Stir gently. Makes about 4 cups (1 L).

1 cup (250 mL): 160 Calories; 1.1 g Total Fat (0.1 g Mono, 0.1 g Poly, 0.6 g Sat); 4 mg Cholesterol; 36 g Carbohydrate; 4 g Fibre; 4 g Protein; 45 mg Sodium

Pictured at right.

Left: Vanilla Fruit Salad, above
Right: Easy Oven-Baked French Toast, page 150
With Mother's Day Breakfast Tray, page 150

Mother's Day Breakfast Tray

Make Mom's breakfast in bed just a little more special by serving it on a tray you've decorated yourself!

MATERIALS
Wooden serving tray
White iridescent latex craft paint
Package of decoupage tissue (or other tissue paper)
Satin finish glue and seal decoupage paste
Cording (optional)

TOOLS
light sandpaper, glue, foam paint brush

Lightly sand the wooden tray so there are no rough edges. Paint the tray inside and out. Let dry. Repeat until covered.

Tear the tissue paper into different sizes and shapes. Using the foam paint brush, apply decoupage paste to the back of the tissue pieces. Attach the tissue pieces to the inside bottom of the tray. Brush over the pieces, smoothing out air bubbles and wrinkles. Apply a final coat of decoupage paste over the inside bottom of the tray once all the pieces are attached and the entire bottom is covered. Let dry.

Measure cording to fit around inside edge of tray and secure with glue to give it a more finished look.

Pictured on page 149.

Thumbprint Box

Show Dad that you aren't all thumbs when it comes to crafting! This isn't only a cute box for holding some very special cookies; it will also make a memorable keepsake.

MATERIALS
Set of acrylic paint cups (primary colors)
Craft box
Colourful ribbon

TOOLS
damp paper towel

Make sure the lids on your paint cups are secure, then tip them upside-down to get some paint on the lid of each cup. Starting with the first colour, press your thumb onto the paint in the lid and then randomly press your thumb onto the box. Repeat with the same colour until you've gone around the entire box. Wipe the paint off your thumb with a damp paper towel. Repeat with the remaining colours of paint until the box is covered with as many thumbprints as you want.

Wrap the ribbon around the box and tie in a bow.

Pictured at right.

Easy Oven-Baked French Toast

You're no fool in the kitchen—Mom has taught you well! So treat Mom and the rest of the family to a special breakfast of French toast on Mother's Day.

Texas bread slices	4	4
Large eggs	4	4
Milk	1 cup	250 mL
Granulated sugar	4 tsp.	20 mL
Ground cinnamon	1 tsp.	5 mL
Vanilla extract	1 tsp.	5 mL
Salt	1/8 tsp.	0.5 mL
Cold butter, cut up	1 tbsp.	15 mL
Icing (confectioner's) sugar, for garnish		

Arrange bread slices in single layer in greased 9 x 9 inch (22 x 22 cm) pan.

Whisk next 6 ingredients in medium bowl. Pour egg mixture evenly over bread slices.

Drop butter pieces randomly over bread. Chill, covered, for about 8 hours or overnight. Bake, uncovered, in 375°F (190°C) oven for about 25 minutes until knife inserted in centre comes out clean.

Sprinkle with icing sugar. Serves 4.

1 serving: 400 Calories; 9.5 g Total Fat (1.0 g Mono, 0.1 g Poly, 4.7 g Sat); 226 mg Cholesterol; 36 g Carbohydrate; 1 g Fibre; 11 g Protein; 405 mg Sodium

Pictured on page 149.

Left: PBJ Thumbprint Cookies, below
Right: Thumbprint Box, left

PBJ Thumbprint Cookies

*Peanut butter and jelly are together forever—
just like you and Dad. Top these cookies with his favourite
flavour of jam and pack them into a Thumbprint Box,
at left, for a really special Father's Day gift.*

Butter (or hard margarine), softened	1/2 cup	125 mL
Brown sugar, packed	1/2 cup	125 mL
Peanut butter	1/2 cup	125 mL
Large egg	1	1
Vanilla extract	1 tsp.	5 mL
All-purpose flour	2 cups	500 mL
Salt	1/2 tsp.	2 mL
Granulated sugar	1/4 cup	60 mL
Grape (or strawberry) jam	1/2 cup	125 mL

Beat first 3 ingredients in large bowl until creamy and smooth. Add egg and vanilla. Beat well.

Combine flour and salt in small bowl. Add to butter mixture in 2 additions, mixing well after each addition until no dry flour remains. Roll into 1 inch (2.5 cm) balls.

Put granulated sugar into small shallow bowl. Roll balls in granulated sugar until coated. Arrange about 1 inch (2.5 cm) apart on greased cookie sheets. Press indentation in centre of each cookie with your thumb.

Fill indentations with about 1/4 tsp. (1 mL) of jam. Bake in 350°F (175°C) oven for about 10 minutes until golden. Let stand on pan for 5 minutes before removing to wire rack to cool completely. Cool cookie sheets between batches. Makes about 45 cookies.

1 cookie: 77 Calories; 3.8 g Total Fat (0.6 g Mono, 0.1 g Poly, 1.7 g Sat); 11 mg Cholesterol; 10 g Carbohydrate; trace Fibre; 1 g Protein; 59 mg Sodium

Pictured above.

Tic-Tac-Toe Tin

Celebrate Grandparents' Day with a special gift and a game you can play together. You can enjoy eating the cookies as you play a game of tic-tac-toe.

MATERIALS
8 1/2 x 11 inch (21 x 28 cm) sheet of orange cardstock
8 1/2 x 11 inch (21 x 28 cm) sheet of purple cardstock
Square metal box or tin, large enough to fit a 6 x 6 inch (15 x 15 cm) board on top
Satin finish glue and seal decoupage paste
Orange wire ribbon (1 1/2 inch, 3.8 cm, wide)
Tic-Tac-Toe Cookies, at right

TOOLS
ruler, pencil, scissors, foam paint brush

Using your ruler, measure and draw five 2 x 2 inch (5 x 5 cm) squares on the orange cardstock. Cut out the squares. Repeat with the purple cardstock, making only 4 squares. Double-check to make sure that three 2 x 2 inch (5 x 5 cm) squares will fit on the lid of your tin. You may have to adjust the size of your squares a little to make them fit.

Using the foam brush, apply a very thin coat of decoupage paste to the back of each square. Glue the squares onto the lid, starting at one side and making a checkerboard pattern across the top of the tin. Let dry. Use the foam brush to apply decoupage paste over the top of your checker board. Follow the directions on the bottle for how long to wait between each coat of paste. Do at least 3 coats. Wipe off any excess paste from the tin using a damp cloth. Let dry overnight.

Fill with orange and purple Tic-Tac-Toe cookies, at right. Wrap the ribbon around the tin and tie in a bow.

Pictured at right.

Favourite Colour Cookies

These crisp sugar cookies aren't only delicious—they're fun too! The dough keeps its shape during baking, so they're perfect for tic-tac-toe or checker pieces that you can eat after the game. Try packing these into the Tic-Tac-Toe Tin, at left, for a special Grandparent's Day gift.

Package of unsweetened drink powder (6 – 8 g, 1/5 – 1/4 oz. size)	1/2	1/2
Salt	1/4 tsp.	1 mL
Water	1 1/2 tsp.	7 mL
Large egg	1	1
Butter (or hard margarine), softened	1/2 cup	125 mL
Granulated sugar	1/2 cup	125 mL
All-purpose flour	1 1/2 cups	375 mL

Stir first 4 ingredients in small bowl until smooth.

Beat butter and sugar in large bowl until light and fluffy. Add egg mixture. Beat until smooth.

Add flour in 2 additions, beating well after each addition until no dry flour remains. Shape into disc. Wrap with plastic wrap. Chill for at least 8 hours or overnight. Let stand at room temperature for 10 minutes. Discard plastic wrap. Roll out dough on lightly floured surface to 1/4 inch (6 mm) thickness. Cut into shapes using lightly floured 2 inch (5 cm) cookie cutters. Roll out scraps to cut more shapes. Arrange, about 1 inch (2.5 cm) apart, on greased cookie sheets. Bake in 350°F (175°C) oven for about 8 minutes until edges start to turn golden. Let stand on cookie sheets for 5 minutes before removing to wire racks to cool. Cool cookie sheets between batches. Makes about 60 cookies.

1 cookie: 32 Calories; 1.6 g Total Fat (0.4 g Mono, 0.1 g Poly, 1.0 g Sat); 6 mg Cholesterol; 4 g Carbohydrate; trace Fibre; trace Protein; 23 mg Sodium

Pictured at right.

Tic-Tac-Toe Cookies: Make dough in 2 batches, using different flavour of drink powder for each half. Use 2 inch (5 cm) cookie cutter to cut out cookies from half of dough. Use different-shaped 2 inch (5 cm) cookie cutter to cut out remaining cookies.

Top: Favourite Colour Cookies, top left, with Tic-Tac-Toe Tin, top right
Bottom: Crispie Cutouts, below

Crispie Cutouts

This is your chance to be a creative cook! These simple treats can be customized for any holiday by using different combinations of cookie cutters and food colourings.

Large marshmallows	33	33
Butter (or hard margarine)	1/4 cup	60 mL
Corn syrup	2 tbsp.	30 mL
Vanilla extract	1 tsp.	5 mL
Drops of liquid food colouring, approximately	10 – 15	10 – 15
Crisp rice cereal	6 cups	1.5 L

Combine first 5 ingredients in Dutch oven. Heat and stir on medium until melted and smooth. Remove from heat.

Add cereal. Stir until combined. Press evenly in greased 10 x 15 inch (25 x 38 cm) baking sheet with sides. Let stand until cool. Cut into shapes using lightly floured 3 inch (7.5 cm) cookie cutters. Makes about 20 cutouts.

1 cutout: 87 Calories; 2.4 g Total Fat (0.6 g Mono, 0.1 g Poly, 1.5 g Sat); 6 mg Cholesterol; 16 g Carbohydrate; trace Fibre; 1 g Protein; 104 mg Sodium

Pictured above.

Lentil Couscous Soup Mix

You may not like to admit it to your friends, but you probably think your teacher is pretty cool. Say a big thank-you for all that he or she does with a package of this yummy soup mix. It's full of warm, Indian flavours that are perfect on a cold, blustery day.

Vegetable bouillon powder	3 tbsp.	50 mL
Parsley flakes	2 tbsp.	30 mL
Onion flakes	1 tbsp.	15 mL
Curry powder	1/2 tsp.	2 mL
Garam masala	1/2 tsp.	2 mL
Salt	1/4 tsp.	1 mL
Whole-wheat couscous	1/2 cup	125 mL
Dehydrated mixed vegetables	1/3 cup	75 mL
Yellow split peas, rinsed and drained	1/3 cup	75 mL
Dried red split lentils	1/3 cup	75 mL
Dried green lentils	1/3 cup	75 mL

Combine first 6 ingredients in small bowl. Spoon into jar with tight-fitting lid.

Layer remaining 5 ingredients, in order given, over spice mixture. Makes about 2 cups (500 mL).

Pictured at right.

Directions for Lentil Couscous Soup:

Bring 8 cups (2 L) water to a boil in large saucepan. Add contents of jar. Stir. Reduce heat to medium-low. Simmer, covered, for about 45 minutes, stirring occasionally, until lentils are tender. Makes about 7 cups (1.75 L).

1 cup (250 mL) soup: 144 Calories; 1.0 g Total Fat (0.1 g Mono, 0.1 g Poly, 0.1 g Sat); 1.1 mg Cholesterol; 26 g Carbohydrate; 4 g Fibre; 9 g Protein; 1513 mg Sodium

---

Painted Chocolate Bar

This one-of-a-kind edible gift is as unique as the artist. So show off your talents and give your teacher an unforgettable gift with this fancy homemade chocolate bar. Candy melting wafers are available in the bulk section of the grocery store, so you can buy small amounts in a variety of colours.

Chocolate melting wafers	2/3 cup	150 mL
Crisp rice cereal	1 tbsp.	15 mL
Toffee bits (such as Skor)	1 tbsp.	15 mL
Green candy melting wafers	1 tbsp.	15 mL
Pink candy melting wafers	1 tbsp.	15 mL
Yellow candy melting wafers	1 tbsp.	15 mL

Put chocolate wafers into small microwave-safe bowl. Microwave, uncovered, on medium (50%), stirring every 15 seconds, until almost melted. Stir until smooth. Spread about 3 tbsp. (50 mL) chocolate evenly in 8 1/2 x 4 1/2 inch (21 x 11 cm) loaf pan to cover bottom.

Sprinkle cereal and toffee bits over chocolate. Chill for 2 minutes. Drizzle remaining melted chocolate over top. Spread evenly. Chill for about 30 minutes until set. Invert loaf pan on work surface. Tap bottom gently to release chocolate bar.

Put green, pink and yellow candy wafers into separate microwave-safe cups (see Tip, below). Microwave each on medium (50%), stirring every 10 seconds, until almost melted. Stir until smooth. Decorate chocolate bar with melted wafers as desired (see Note). Makes 1 large chocolate bar.

1 bar: 1033 Calories; 64.9 g Total Fat (4.1 g Mono, 0.5 g Poly, 36.8 g Sat); 16 mg Cholesterol; 127 g Carbohydrate; 10 g Fibre; 13 g Protein; 167 mg Sodium

Pictured at right.

Note: Use a paint brush to decorate bar, or transfer melted wafers to small resealable freezer bag. Snip tiny piece off one corner and pipe design on chocolate bar. To give yourself plenty of painting time, set small bowls of melted candy wafers in a dish of hot water.

Variation: Stir the cereal and toffee bits right into the chocolate. The top will be a little bumpy, but it will be easier for small children to work with.

Tip: Reheat dipping chocolate and candy in microwave for 30 seconds if it cools and starts to harden.

Top Left: Lentil Couscous Soup Mix, this page
Top Right: Caramel Candy Apples, right
Bottom: Painted Chocolate Bar, above

Caramel Candy Apples

This classic teacher's gift is made even sweeter with the addition of a sticky caramel coating and colourful candies! The perfect gift for a really fun teacher.

Small unpeeled tart apples (such as Granny Smith), blossom and stem removed	4	4
Freezer pop sticks	4	4
Bag of caramels (about 40), unwrapped	12 oz.	340 g
Water	1 tbsp.	15 mL
Candy sprinkles (or confetti spinkles or toasted finely chopped nuts, see Tip, page 141)	3 tbsp.	50 mL

Insert freezer pop stick into centre of each apple at stem end.

Combine caramels and water in small microwave-safe bowl. Microwave on high (100%) for about 3 minutes until almost melted. Stir until smooth. Place 1 apple in caramel mixture. Spoon caramel over apple until coated, scraping excess from bottom of apple back into bowl. Place, stick-side up, on parchment paper-lined baking sheet. Repeat with remaining apples and caramel (see Note). Chill, uncovered, for at least 8 hours or overnight. Caramel will be set but still slightly sticky.

Measure sprinkles into shallow dish. Roll caramel-coated apples in sprinkles until completely coated. Makes 4 caramel apples.

1 apple: 411 Calories; 8.6 g Total Fat (1.2 g Mono, 2.7 g Poly, 3.4 g Sat); 9 mg Cholesterol; 85 g Carbohydrate; 3 g Fibre; 5 g Protein; 200 mg Sodium

Pictured on page 144 and below.

Note: If caramel becomes too thick to coat apples, reheat in microwave on high (100%) for about 20 seconds.

Wrap It Up

Add the perfect finishing touches to all your gifts with these handy ideas for turning delicious food into perfect presents. Simple ideas for bows, bags, wrapping and gift boxes elevate home-cooked goodies into elegant and impressive gifts. These craft projects add a whole bunch of personality and a tonne of fun to your kitchen gifts.

From Left to Right: Photo Flip Card, page 163; Orange-Spiced Honey, page 9, with Bee Mine Tag, below; File Folder Card, page 163; Burning Love Spice Rub, page 103

How To

Bee Mine Tag

There'll be no question who your Valentine is when you attach this cute tag to a homemade gift, made especially for your sweetheart.

MATERIALS
Purple craft foam
2 pieces of pink chenille stem (3 inch, 7.5 cm, length)
Piece of purple chenille stem (3 inch, 7.5 cm, length)

TOOLS
scissors, pencil, needle nose pliers, low temperature glue gun, black, purple and red markers

Trace the pattern pieces onto the purple craft foam. Cut out the pieces.

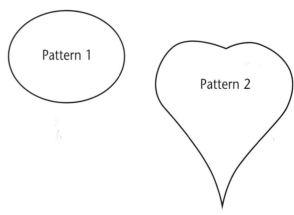

Twist the ends of 1 pink chenille stem together with pliers. Use the pliers to pull down the middle of the loop to shape into a heart. Repeat with the remaining pink chenille stem. These are the wings. Shape the purple chenille stem into antennas.

Glue the head of the bee (Pattern 1) to the body (Pattern 2). Glue the antennas and the wings to the back of the body. Using the markers, draw stripes and a face and write "Bee Mine" on the bee.

Pictured above.

How To

Bow-Making 101

This makes a four-loop bow, but you can adapt these simple instructions to make any size bow you like—just add more loops for a bigger bow. With a little practice, you'll be an expert at bow-making in no time.

MATERIALS
Florist wire or chenille stems
Ribbon

TOOLS
wire cutters, scissors

Cut a 6 inch (15 cm) piece of wire with wire cutters. Cut a 32 inch (80 cm) length of ribbon. Pinch between thumb and forefinger, 3 1/2 inches (9 cm) from 1 end. Make a 1 1/2 inch (3.8 cm) loop with 3 inches (7.5 cm) of ribbon and pinch tightly. Twist ribbon at the pinch. Make another 1 1/2 inch (3.8 cm) loop on the other side. Make a centre loop, forming a small loop over your thumb. Pinch and twist (see photo).

Using the same method, make 1 more loop per side. Thread the wire through the centre loop of the bow and wrap around the twisted centre portion. Twist wire tightly at the back of the bow to secure. Fluff out bow loops. Cut the tail ends of the ribbon as desired.

Variations: Try layering 2 bows for a multicoloured bow. Just place a bow without a middle loop on the bottom and tie the two bows together.

6-loop bow with no middle pictured on page 107.

6-loop bow with middle pictured on page 105.

How To

Bottleneck Ribbon Ring

This is a nice way to glitz up a bottle of homemade liqueur for your New Year's party hostess.

MATERIALS
Metal ring (2 1/2 inch, 6.4 cm, diameter)
7 pieces of sheer blue ribbon (5/8 inch, 1.5 cm, wide),
   12 inches (30 cm) long
7 pieces of sheer silver ribbon (5/8 inch, 1.5 cm, wide),
   10 inches (25 cm) long
14 beads for blue ribbon
14 beads for silver ribbon

TOOLS
needle (with long, narrow eye), scissors

Tie the centre of one blue ribbon to the ring, leaving two ends of equal length. Repeat with the remaining ribbons, alternating between blue and silver.

Make sure that both the needle and the ribbon will fit through the hole in the beads. Thread the end of 1 ribbon through the eye of the needle and thread through a bead. Tie a knot at the end of the ribbon to secure the bead. Repeat with remaining ribbons and beads. Cut off any loose ends of ribbon, just below the bead and knot. Arrange the ribbons evenly around the metal ring.

Pictured at right and on page 97.

Clockwise from Top:
Flower Bottle Topper, page 94
Vanilla Brandy Liqueur, page 36
Summer Herb Dressing, page 117
Canadiana Liqueur, page 96, with Bottleneck Ribbon Ring, left

Hot Chocolate Gift Packages

We've used this as a convenient package to hold hot chocolate mix for a wedding favour. But this easy packaging can be used for any occasion—just use any colours of cardstock and ribbon to suit your event.

MATERIALS

Dry hot chocolate mix (about 5 1/4 cups, 1.3 L)
12 small resealable plastic bags (3 x 4 inch, 7.5 x 10 cm, each), or snack-sized
Twelve 10 1/2 x 3 1/2 inch (26 x 9 cm) pieces of cardstock
Embellishments
12 small pieces of paper
12 pieces of ribbon (1/4 inch, 6 mm, wide), 9 inches, (22 cm) long

TOOLS

paper trimmer, hole punch

Put about 7 tbsp (105 mL) hot chocolate mix into each plastic bag. If you are using snack-sized bags, fold the bags in half to make them smaller.

Take 1 of the 10 1/2 x 3 1/2 inch (26 x 9 cm) pieces of cardstock. Measuring from the left edge and paying attention to which direction the folds are being made, make folds at the following intervals (see photo):

1 inch (2.5 cm)

5 inches (12.5 cm)

5 3/4 inches (14.5 cm)

6 1/2 inches (16.2 cm)

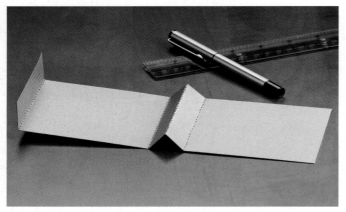

Decorate the package with embellishments to suit the occasion and theme. Stamps, heart-shaped brads, cardstock in different colours and thank-you tags work well for a wedding favour. On a piece of paper, write directions for preparing the mix, and tape to back of plastic bag inside the package.

Place the hot chocolate bag inside of the package with the top of the plastic bag inside the 1 inch (2.5 cm) fold. Using the hole punch, make 2 holes in the centre of the 1 inch (2.5 cm) flap, about 1/4 inch (6 mm) apart, making sure to include the plastic bag. Tie with the pieces of ribbon. Repeat with remaining materials to make a total of 12 hot chocolate packages.

Pictured on pages 4 and 69 and at right.

```
┌─────────────────────┐
│                     │
│     1" (2.5 cm)     │
│ - - - - - - - - - - │
│                     │
│                     │
│                     │
│    5" (12.5 cm)     │
│ - - - - - - - - - - │
│  5 3/4" (14.5 cm)   │
│ - - - - - - - - - - │
│   6 1/2" (16.2 cm)  │
│ - - - - - - - - - - │
│                     │
│                     │
│                     │
│                     │
│                     │
│                     │
└─────────────────────┘
```

Birthday Loot Bag

Instead of using plastic loot bags that just get thrown away, the kids can take these home at the end of the party and reuse them. This pattern is for a girl's bag, but you could easily vary the colour and decoration for a boy's birthday party.

MATERIALS
9 x 12 inch (22 x 30 cm) piece of brightly coloured felt
Thread to match
Scrap pieces of felt for flowers
Colourful brads

TOOLS
pins, scissors, sewing machine, seam ripper

Enlarge patterns by 200%. This loot bag is sewn so that the seams are to the outside of the bag. The seam allowance is 1/4 inch (6 mm) unless otherwise stated.

Cut 1 bottom (Pattern 1), 2 sides (Pattern 2) and 2 front/back pieces (Pattern 3) from the sheet of felt. Pin the 3 inch (7.5 cm) side of bottom to 1 end of each side piece. Sew, starting and ending (see photo 1) 1/4 inch (6 mm) from the ends. Repeat on other side.

Pin 1 front/back piece to the sides and bottom of bag. Stitch the front and back to the sides and bottom.

Cut 2 flower petal pieces (Pattern 4), and 1 flower middle (Pattern 5), each from a different colour of felt. Take 1 petal piece and fold it in half. Pin 1/2 inch (12 mm) from edge on both sides (see photo 2). Sew between the pins, close to the fold, and don't forget to back stitch. Fold the flower in half the other way, pin, and repeat sewing. Repeat with the other petal piece. Follow the same instructions for middle, placing pins 1/8 inch (3 mm) from edge.

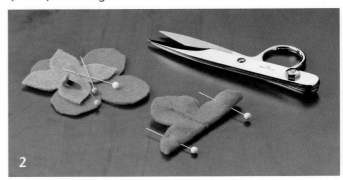

Use the seam ripper to carefully make a small hole at the centre of each piece where the threads cross. Insert the brad through the hole in the middle piece, following with the two petal pieces, staggering the petals of each flower slightly. Mark where the flower will be attached to the bag. Use the seam ripper to make a small hole in the bag. Attach the flower and open the brad inside the bag to secure.

4 1/2" (11 cm)

Pattern 1

3" (7.5 cm)

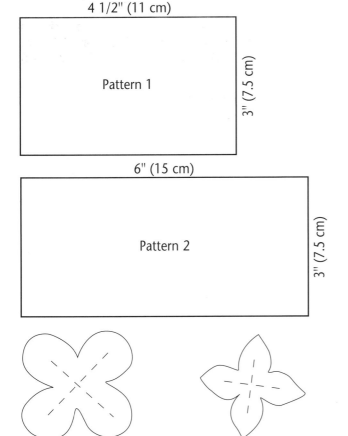

6" (15 cm)

Pattern 2

3" (7.5 cm)

6" (15 cm)

Pattern 3

4 1/2" (11 cm)

Pattern 4

Pattern 5

How To

Photo Flip Card

Give Mom a truly personalized card this Mother's Day. Decorate the card with your own photo and a personal sentiment for a special keepsake.

MATERIALS
4 1/2 x 5 inch (11 x 12.5 cm) piece of cardstock
2 x 2 inch (5 x 5 cm) photo
Embellishments, such as stickers, beads, flowers (optional)

TOOLS
ruler, pencil, paper trimmer or scissors, eraser, photo-safe glue or double-sided tape, pen

Place the cardstock so that the 5 inch (12.5 cm) side is facing you at the top and bottom. With your ruler, mark and draw a dotted line to 1 inch (2.5 cm) down from the edge, at 2 inches (5 cm) and 3 inches (7.5 cm). Repeat on the bottom of the paper using the same measurements (see diagram). Draw a 1 inch (2.5 cm) border around the paper, from one dotted line to the other, on both sides. Use the paper trimmer or scissors and cut on the solid lines only.

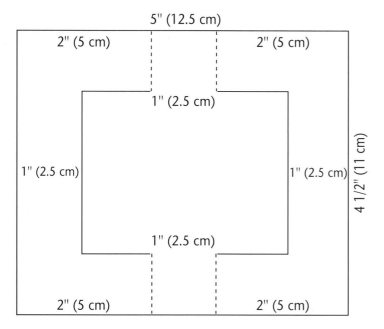

Turn the cardstock so the 4 1/2 inch (11 cm) side is facing you. Fold the nearest side towards the centre along the dotted line. Do not fold centre rectangle. Flip card over. Fold the opposite side towards the centre. It will look like an accordion. Erase pencil markings.

Glue the photo to 1 side of the centre rectangle. On the opposite side of the card, you can write a message to Mom. Decorate the card with embellishments as desired.

Pictured on pages 23 and 157.

How To

File Folder Card

Show your administrative assistant just how much his or her hard work is appreciated with this homemade card attached to a package of goodies.

MATERIALS
8 1/2 x 11 inch (21 x 28 cm) piece of cardstock
Office-themed embellishments

TOOLS
fine black pen, paper trimmer, scissors, glue, ruler

Enlarge Pattern 1 by 200%. Trace onto cardstock. Cut on solid lines. Fold card on dotted line. Print "V is for Valuable" on the tab. Decorate the front of the card with the embellishments.

Pictured on pages 19 and 157.

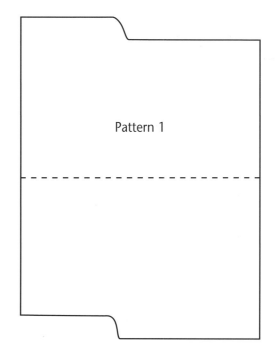

Pattern 1

Crafty Recycling

You think packaging up your homemade gifts has to be expensive? Rubbish! The truth is, there are valuable crafting materials right in your recycle bin! There are all sorts of crafting possibilities for those empty cereal boxes, containers, cans and newspapers.

Not only does reusing or recycling save you money on craft supplies, it's also great for the environment. Recycling is becoming a part of the way people live, so why shouldn't it be a part of the way people craft?

We have created a few special craft projects that use recycled materials; however, many arts and crafts projects can be made with extra cardboard or materials that you've got lying around. You just need to use your imagination! Old cardboard boxes can be easily recovered with colourful paper, metal cans can be painted over and plastic containers can be washed and decorated for transporting your tasty kitchen treats. You can even cover your work table with old newspapers instead of a clean sheet of paper to make cleanup a breeze. Once you're done, just put the newspapers back in the recycle bin—now you've found another use for something that would have been recycled anyways! And this way you don't have to use harsh cleaners to get any paint or glue off your work table.

After you've added all your special touches and decorations, it's unlikely that the lucky recipients of your kitchen gifts will even notice that you've reused materials. And if they do, they will be very impressed with your creativity and environmental concern. So refuse to waste, and get in on the recycling revolution!

How To

Bento Gift Box

Recycling is an excellent way to curb waste. Show that you care about the environment by packaging a special gift in a reused cereal box—all dressed up like a bento box! This gift doesn't just show that you care about the recipient; it shows that you care about making the world a better and cleaner place.

MATERIALS
Small cereal (or similar-shaped) box
Wrapping paper
Ribbon

TOOLS
scissors, tape, ruler

Tape box ends closed. Lay the box on its side and cut out the top to make a tray. You will be using the piece you are cutting out so try to cut as close to the edges as possible. Wrap the box with wrapping paper. Tie a ribbon around the sides of the box in a bow.

Measure out different compartment sizes, keeping in mind the sizes of the items you are placing in the box. Cut out your dividers from the piece of cardboard you removed from the top of your tray. Cover the dividers with wrapping paper. Place the dividers snugly in the box.

Pictured on pages 79 and 167.

How To

School Bus Gift Box

Don't forget the person who drives the children safely to school each day! This is a fun package to give your bus driver, especially when it is filled with homemade goodies.

MATERIALS
Shoe box with lid
Extra shoe box lid (same size)
Yellow, grey and black paper
4 large silver brads

TOOLS
ruler, scissors, pencil, fast-grab tacky glue, tape, sharp
  object (like a small screwdriver), black marker

On the narrow end of the shoe box, cut halfway down on both corners. Fold this piece into the box at a 45° angle. Mark on the inside of the box where this piece ends. Cut straight down the long side of the box to the mark you made (see photo). Repeat on the other side. Fold these flaps in under the front flap and glue or tape to secure.

Place the lid on top, mark with the ruler where the windshield starts and draw a line across the lid. Cut along this line to take the end of the lid off. Save this piece for the bumper. Take the extra lid and cut four 2 inch (5 cm) diameter circles for the wheels. Cut a 1 inch (2.5 cm) piece off the short end of the lid to make the second bumper.

To make the windshield, measure the opening in the front and add 2 inches (5 cm) to the length and 1 inch (2.5 cm) to the width. Cut the grey paper as measured and fold 1 inch (2.5 cm) flaps on each narrow side. Cut 1 inch (2.5 cm) up on each flap. Slide the middle of the windshield down into the bus. Glue 1 inch (2.5 cm) flaps to the outside of bus.

Wrap the box and the lid with the yellow paper. Cover the bumpers and wheels with the black paper. Cut several 1/2 inch (1.25 cm) thick strips from the black paper. Cut square windows and a rectangle door from the grey paper.

Attach the bumpers to the bus with glue. Find the right position for the wheels. Poke a small hole, as close to the bottom of the box as possible, with a sharp object. Poke a hole through the centre of each wheel. Insert the brad through the wheel and into the box. Open the brad inside the box to secure. Glue the windows, door and black strips onto the bus. Use the marker to number your bus or write the school's name on the side.

Pictured at right and on page 81.

Top: School Bus Box, above
Bottom Left: Green Tea Shortbread, page 79
Bottom Right: Soothing Green Tea Blend, page 79
With Bento Gift Box, page 164

Measurement Tables

Throughout this book, measurements are given in Conventional and Metric measure. To compensate for differences between the two measurements due to rounding, a full metric measure is not always used. The cup used is the standard 8 fluid ounce. Temperature is given in degrees Fahrenheit and Celsius. Baking pan measurements are in inches and centimetres as well as quarts and litres. An exact metric conversion is given on this page as well as the working equivalent (Metric Standard Measure).

Left: Caramel Pecan Fudge, page 100
Right: Triple Chocolate Cookie Mix, page 100

Oven Temperatures

Fahrenheit (°F)	Celsius (°C)	Fahrenheit (°F)	Celsius (°C)
175°	80°	350°	175°
200°	95°	375°	190°
225°	110°	400°	205°
250°	120°	425°	220°
275°	140°	450°	230°
300°	150°	475°	240°
325°	160°	500°	260°

Spoons

Conventional Measure	Metric Exact Conversion Millilitre (mL)	Metric Standard Measure Millilitre (mL)
1/8 teaspoon (tsp.)	0.6 mL	0.5 mL
1/4 teaspoon (tsp.)	1.2 mL	1 mL
1/2 teaspoon (tsp.)	2.4 mL	2 mL
1 teaspoon (tsp.)	4.7 mL	5 mL
2 teaspoons (tsp.)	9.4 mL	10 mL
1 tablespoon (tbsp.)	14.2 mL	15 mL

Cups

1/4 cup (4 tbsp.)	56.8 mL	60 mL
1/3 cup (5 1/3 tbsp.)	75.6 mL	75 mL
1/2 cup (8 tbsp.)	113.7 mL	125 mL
2/3 cup (10 2/3 tbsp.)	151.2 mL	150 mL
3/4 cup (12 tbsp.)	170.5 mL	175 mL
1 cup (16 tbsp.)	227.3 mL	250 mL
4 1/2 cups	1022.9 mL	1000 mL (1 L)

Pans

Conventional Inches	Metric Centimetres
8 x 8 inch	20 x 20 cm
9 x 9 inch	22 x 22 cm
9 x 13 inch	22 x 33 cm
10 x 15 inch	25 x 38 cm
11 x 17 inch	28 x 43 cm
8 x 2 inch round	20 x 5 cm
9 x 2 inch round	22 x 5 cm
10 x 4 1/2 inch tube	25 x 11 cm
8 x 4 x 3 inch loaf	20 x 10 x 7.5 cm
9 x 5 x 3 inch loaf	22 x 12.5 x 7.5 cm

Dry Measurements

Conventional Measure Ounces (oz.)	Metric Exact Conversion Grams (g)	Metric Standard Measure Grams (g)
1 oz.	28.3 g	28 g
2 oz.	56.7 g	57 g
3 oz.	85.0 g	85 g
4 oz.	113.4 g	125 g
5 oz.	141.7 g	140 g
6 oz.	170.1 g	170 g
7 oz.	198.4 g	200 g
8 oz.	226.8 g	250 g
16 oz.	453.6 g	500 g
32 oz.	907.2 g	1000 g (1 kg)

Casseroles

Canada & Britain		United States	
Standard Size Casserole	Exact Metric Measure	Standard Size Casserole	Exact Metric Measure
1 qt. (5 cups)	1.13 L	1 qt. (4 cups)	900 mL
1 1/2 qts. (7 1/2 cups)	1.69 L	1 1/2 qts. (6 cups)	1.35 L
2 qts. (10 cups)	2.25 L	2 qts. (8 cups)	1.8 L
2 1/2 qts. (12 1/2 cups)	2.81 L	2 1/2 qts. (10 cups)	2.25 L
3 qts. (15 cups)	3.38 L	3 qts. (12 cups)	2.7 L
4 qts. (20 cups)	4.5 L	4 qts. (16 cups)	3.6 L
5 qts. (25 cups)	5.63 L	5 qts. (20 cups)	4.5 L

How-To Index

Tip Index

Recipe Index

"The last bite tasted is
the first one remembered."

Jean Paré